Haunted Hospitals

Ghostly Encounters and Paranormal Phenomena

in Medical Facilities

By Lee Brickley

Contents:

Introduction..5
The Waverly Hills Sanatorium...................................11
Rolling Hills Asylum..17
Trans-Allegheny Lunatic Asylum...............................23
Old Changi Hospital..29
Beechworth Lunatic Asylum......................................35
Aradale Mental Hospital..41
Taunton State Hospital..47
Poveglia Island..53
Severalls Hospital..59
Gonjiam Psychiatric Hospital.....................................63
St. Albans Sanatorium...71
Pennhurst Asylum...77
Royal Hope Hospital..83
Hirosaki City Hospital...89
Linda Vista Hospital..95

Denbigh Mental Asylum	101
The Athens Lunatic Asylum	107
Edinburgh's Royal Hospital for Sick Children	113
Sai Ying Pun Psychiatry Hospital	119
Lier Sykehus	125
Afterword	133

Introduction

Within the depths of human consciousness, the fear of the unknown, the mysterious, and the inexplicable has persisted throughout the ages. Haunted hospitals, with their eerie corridors and spine-chilling histories, lie at the crossroads of life and death, where the veil between the worlds grows thin. "Haunted Hospitals: Ghostly Encounters and Paranormal Phenomena in Medical Facilities" invites you on an unsettling journey into the shadowy realms of medical institutions across the globe, where the veil between the living and the dead is said to be at its thinnest, and supernatural occurrences abound.

As you step into the pages of this haunting tome, you will explore the chilling past of medical facilities that were once dedicated to the healing of the body and mind, but now serve as harbingers of paranormal activity and ghostly encounters. These once-thriving hubs of medicine have become eerie reminders of human suffering and anguish, with the spirits of former patients and staff said to linger in the forgotten corners of these desolate buildings.

Your journey begins with the Waverly Hills Sanatorium, a former tuberculosis hospital in Kentucky, where spectral activity and disquieting voices have become the norm. This unnerving account sets the stage for the thrilling tales that await, as we delve into the ghostly world of haunted hospitals and asylums, where the tormented souls of those who suffered in life are believed to roam as restless spirits in the afterlife.

As you traverse through the dark annals of haunted medical facilities, you will encounter the unseen residents of Rolling Hills Asylum in New York, where the infamous "Shadow People" are said to lurk alongside the tormented spirits of former patients. Unravel the chilling stories of Trans-Allegheny Lunatic Asylum in West Virginia, where ghostly nurses and patients who never left the premises are rumoured to haunt the once-bustling institution.

Embark on a global expedition into the realm of the paranormal, as you discover the sinister sanctuary of Old Changi Hospital in Singapore, a World War II-era facility still haunted by the restless spirits and wartime horrors of its past. Wander the haunted shores of Poveglia Island in Italy, where the tormented souls of plague victims are said to linger within the decaying hospital buildings.

Journey through the unsettling halls of madness at Aradale Mental Hospital in Australia, where dark secrets and restless spirits continue to haunt its abandoned wards. Explore the eerie remnants of Taunton State Hospital in Massachusetts, where shadowy figures and ghostly patients have been witnessed roaming the halls.

Throughout this spine-chilling compendium, you will encounter the supernatural phenomena that lurk within the haunted institutions of various countries, from the ghostly inhabitants of England's Severalls Hospital to the haunted house of horrors that is South Korea's Gonjiam Psychiatric Hospital. Traverse the haunted landscapes of St. Albans Sanatorium in Virginia, where unexplained phenomena and chilling encounters plague the historic former hospital.

Uncover the paranormal mysteries of Hirosaki City Hospital in Japan, a historic medical facility with a reputation for ghostly patients and unexplained encounters. Investigate the chilling tales of wandering spirits and ghostly nurses that haunt the halls of Royal Hope Hospital in Florida, a former military hospital with a troubled past.

As you delve deeper into these haunting stories, you will discover the tragic history and ghostly encounters that continue to echo through the abandoned wards of Denbigh Mental Asylum in Wales. Explore the supernatural occurrences at the Athens Lunatic Asylum in Ohio, a former mental health facility now part of Ohio University. Unravel the intriguing tales of healing spirits and paranormal encounters at Edinburgh's Royal Hospital for Sick Children in Scotland.

Finally, venture into the forsaken halls of Lier Sykehus in Norway, an abandoned asylum of shadows, where the chilling past and paranormal phenomena continue to mystify visitors who dare to enter its confines. Here, restless spirits and unnerving encounters serve as a stark reminder of the suffering that once permeated the walls of this forsaken institution.

As you immerse yourself in "Haunted Hospitals: Ghostly Encounters and Paranormal Phenomena in Medical Facilities," you will find yourself transported to the eerie, hallowed halls of these once-vibrant institutions. With each turn of the page, you will uncover the dark histories and chilling tales that have transformed these medical facilities into harbingers of the supernatural, where ghostly apparitions and inexplicable occurrences have become the norm.

Prepare yourself for a spine-tingling journey into the shadowy world of haunted hospitals and asylums, where the lines between life and death, the natural and the supernatural, blur beyond recognition. Uncover the chilling secrets that lie within the abandoned wards of these once-revered medical facilities, and delve deep into the world of the unknown, where the spirits of those who once sought healing and solace continue to roam, restless and unseen.

The Waverly Hills Sanatorium

Perched atop a hill in Louisville, Kentucky, the Waverly Hills Sanatorium looms ominously, its shadow stretching across the landscape like a spectral hand. As a former tuberculosis hospital, it has seen its fair share of suffering, and the energy left behind has made it an epicentre of ghostly activity. Today, the sanatorium is a popular destination for paranormal investigators, and its chilling history has captivated the imagination of countless visitors.

The hospital was built in the early 20th century, during a time when tuberculosis was rampant throughout the United States. The sanatorium was designed to isolate patients from the general population in an attempt to curb the spread of the disease. Over the years, thousands of patients passed through its doors, and many succumbed to the deadly illness. The sheer amount of death and despair that took place within the hospital's walls has left a lasting imprint, and the sanatorium has become infamous for its frequent paranormal sightings and events.

One of the most well-known apparitions reported at Waverly Hills is the ghost of a nurse who is said to have taken her own life in Room 502. Staff and visitors alike have reported witnessing her melancholy spirit wandering the halls, dressed in her white nurse's uniform. Her presence is accompanied by a palpable sense of sadness, and many who have encountered her claim to have felt an overwhelming sense of despair.

Visitors to the sanatorium have also reported seeing the ghost of a young boy, affectionately referred to as "Timmy." It is believed that Timmy was a patient at the hospital who died from tuberculosis. His playful spirit is said to roam the halls, often rolling a ball towards those who are open to communicating with him. Paranormal investigators have captured recordings of a child's voice, and many believe it to be the voice of Timmy reaching out from beyond the grave.

Another chilling presence that has been reported throughout the sanatorium is the ghost of a man wearing a white coat and carrying a clipboard. Some speculate that he may have been a doctor who worked at the facility, while others believe he could have been a patient who wore a white coat to feel more in control of his situation. Regardless of his identity, his presence has been described as unnerving and unsettling, and many claim that he appears to be checking on patients that no longer occupy the now-empty rooms.

One of the most notorious and disturbing areas of the sanatorium is the infamous "death tunnel" or "body chute." This 500-foot-long tunnel was used to transport the bodies of deceased patients from the hospital to a waiting hearse at the bottom of the hill. The tunnel allowed the staff to remove the bodies discreetly, without causing distress to the other patients. Today, the death tunnel is said to be haunted by the souls of the countless individuals whose remains were transported through it. Visitors have reported hearing footsteps echoing through the tunnel, as well as disembodied voices whispering in the darkness.

Over the years, there have been countless firsthand accounts of paranormal activity at the Waverly Hills Sanatorium. One such account comes from a man named John, who visited the facility as part of a ghost tour. As he wandered the darkened halls, he was suddenly overcome with a sense of dread, as if he were being watched. He turned a corner and came face-to-face with the apparition of a woman, who seemed to be beckoning him towards her. As he approached, the figure vanished, leaving him shaken and bewildered.

Another visitor, Susan, recalled her unnerving encounter with the spirit of a young girl on the third floor. As she stood in the dimly lit hallway, she noticed a small figure standing at the end of the corridor, clutching a tattered doll. As Susan moved closer, the girl's transparent form became clearer, and she realised that the child's eyes were filled with sorrow. Susan attempted to communicate with the spirit, asking her name and if she needed help. The young girl didn't respond, but her gaze remained fixed on Susan. Suddenly, the girl turned and disappeared through a closed door, leaving Susan with a chilling memory of her ghostly encounter.

Eyewitness accounts of unexplained phenomena at Waverly Hills are not limited to visual sightings. Many visitors have reported inexplicable cold spots, sudden drops in temperature that seemingly defy logic. Others have experienced being touched or pushed by unseen hands, and some have even reported hearing their names being whispered in the empty halls. Investigators have captured countless EVPs (Electronic Voice Phenomena) within the sanatorium, with disembodied voices ranging from faint whispers to anguished cries.

One particularly harrowing account comes from a paranormal investigator named Mark. As he conducted an EVP session in the basement, he asked if any spirits wished to communicate. Moments later, he felt a cold breeze pass through him, and his audio equipment captured a chilling, guttural growl that seemed to emanate from the darkness. Shaken, Mark quickly left the basement, convinced that he had made contact with a malevolent presence.

The Waverly Hills Sanatorium's chilling history and countless eyewitness accounts have cemented its reputation as one of the most haunted locations in the world. The spirits of former patients and staff are believed to be trapped within the hospital's walls, forever bound to the place where they experienced so much pain and suffering.

As visitors continue to seek answers to the mysteries that surround the Waverly Hills Sanatorium, they are left with more questions than resolutions. The lingering energy of the building's tragic past continues to draw those who are fascinated by the unknown, and the countless souls who are said to haunt its halls remain restless and unseen. Perhaps one day, the spirits of

Waverly Hills will find peace, but for now, their stories continue to haunt the living, serving as a chilling testament to the power of the paranormal.

In the end, the Waverly Hills Sanatorium remains a breeding ground for spectral activity, where ghostly apparitions and chilling voices continue to captivate those who dare to enter its hallowed halls.

Rolling Hills Asylum

In the middle of rural New York, shrouded by the shadows of the surrounding woodland, lies the desolate and decaying Rolling Hills Asylum. Once a thriving medical institution, it now stands as a testament to human suffering and anguish. Its dark past has given rise to countless tales of tormented spirits who are said to roam its abandoned halls and the enigmatic "Shadow People" who are encountered by those who dare to venture within.

The asylum's history dates back to the early 19th century, when it was established as the Genesee County Poor Farm. It was a place where society's outcasts— the poor, the mentally ill, orphans, and widows— could find shelter and work. As the needs of the community changed, so too did the institution. Over the years, it evolved into a nursing home, a tuberculosis hospital, and eventually an asylum for the mentally ill.

The suffering endured by those who called Rolling Hills Asylum home has left an indelible mark on its very fabric, with numerous reports of paranormal activity within its walls. Those who have ventured inside have encountered spectral figures, disembodied voices, and the eerie sensation of being watched by unseen eyes.

One of the most notorious spirits said to haunt Rolling Hills Asylum is that of Roy Crouse, a former patient who suffered from gigantism. Standing at over seven feet tall, Roy's imposing presence can still be felt throughout the building. Visitors have reported feeling his large, cold hand on their shoulder, only to turn around and find no one there. In the asylum's solitary confinement wing, Roy's disembodied voice has been captured on numerous EVP recordings, seemingly pleading for help or company.

Another tormented soul believed to haunt the asylum is that of Nurse Emma, a dedicated caregiver who worked tirelessly to tend to the needs of the patients. Tragically, she took her own life within the confines of the hospital, unable to cope with the immense suffering that surrounded her. To this day, her ghost is said to wander the halls, clad in her white nurse's uniform, tending to the spirits of those who never left the asylum. Her perfume is said to linger in the air, a subtle reminder of her continued presence.

Yet, it is the enigmatic "Shadow People" that make Rolling Hills Asylum truly unique among haunted locations. These elusive entities are often described as dark, human-shaped figures that appear to be composed of pure shadow. They have been reported to move with incredible speed, flitting through the hallways, and disappearing as suddenly as they appear. Their intentions remain a mystery, as they seem to be neither benevolent nor malevolent, simply existing within the realm of the unknown.

Over the years, countless paranormal investigators have ventured into the asylum, armed with an array of high-tech equipment in an attempt to document the supernatural phenomena that pervade its halls. One such investigator, named John, had a chilling encounter with one of the infamous "Shadow People." As he walked through a dimly lit corridor, he suddenly felt a cold breeze pass through his body. Turning around, he found himself face to face with a towering, shadowy figure. The entity stared at him intently for a moment before vanishing into thin air, leaving John shaken and questioning the nature of the unseen world.

Another investigator, Sarah, had a heart-wrenching experience in the former children's ward. As she explored the area, she was suddenly overcome by a profound sadness and could hear the faint sounds of children sobbing. She felt an overwhelming sense of despair, as if she was experiencing the sorrow of the countless young souls who had suffered within the asylum's walls.

Rolling Hills Asylum's chilling past and the countless ghostly encounters that have been reported within its walls have made it a place of great interest to those fascinated by the paranormal. The tormented spirits that are said to roam the abandoned halls serve as a haunting reminder of the suffering that once permeated the asylum.

One particularly disturbing account comes from a visitor named Linda, who decided to explore the former operating room. As she entered the dimly lit space, the atmosphere grew heavy, and she felt a sudden wave of nausea wash over her. Sensing a presence nearby, Linda turned to see a spectral surgeon, clad in blood-stained scrubs, standing over the ghostly figure of a patient on the operating table. The horrifying scene played out before her eyes, and she could hear the agonising screams of the patient. Overcome by the intensity of the encounter, Linda fled the room, shaken by what she had witnessed.

The asylum's morgue is another area that has been the site of numerous paranormal experiences. One chilling account comes from an investigator named Mark, who found himself drawn to the cold, sterile room during a late-night exploration of the asylum. As he stood among the empty gurneys and rusted medical equipment, Mark felt a sudden chill in the air. A disembodied voice whispered his name, and he felt a cold hand grasp his shoulder. The sensation of being watched by unseen eyes grew overwhelming, and Mark quickly made his way out of the morgue, unable to shake the feeling that the spirits of the deceased were reaching out to him from beyond the grave.

In addition to the countless personal experiences reported by those who have ventured within Rolling Hills Asylum, paranormal investigators have captured a wealth of compelling evidence of the supernatural phenomena that pervades the building. From ghostly apparitions and unexplained shadows caught on film to chilling EVP recordings of disembodied voices, the asylum has become a treasure trove for those seeking to explore the mysteries of the unknown.

The haunting legacy of Rolling Hills Asylum has left a profound impact on those who have dared to explore its abandoned ha From the tormented spirits who are said to roam the buildi the enigmatic "Shadow People" who lurk within its shadows, the asylum has become a breeding ground for paranormal activity. As visitors traverse the once-bustling corridors, they are left to ponder the nature of the unseen world that exists just beyond our perception, where the spirits of those who once sought solace within the asylum's walls continue to roam, restless and unseen.

For those who dare to step into the darkness of Rolling Hills Asylum, the chilling encounters and ghostly tales serve as a stark reminder of the suffering that once took place within its walls. The asylum stands as a testament to the pain and anguish of its former residents, and the paranormal phenomena that continues to occur within its confines beckons to those who are brave enough to explore the realm of the unknown. With each new encounter and piece of evidence captured, the mysteries of Rolling Hills Asylum continue to captivate and intrigue those who seek answers to the age-old questions of life, death, and the world that lies beyond our understanding.

Trans-Allegheny Lunatic Asylum

In the heart of West Virginia, the Trans-Allegheny Lunatic Asylum stands as a haunting testament to the pain and suffering experienced by countless individuals within its walls. Built during the mid-19th century, the asylum was designed to house the mentally ill and provide them with the care and treatment they desperately needed. However, as time went on, the facility became plagued by overcrowding, abuse, and neglect, ultimately leading to its closure in the 1990s. Today, the asylum is a popular destination for paranormal enthusiasts and ghost hunters, who seek to uncover the stories of the tortured souls that continue to haunt its dark and foreboding halls.

The Trans-Allegheny Lunatic Asylum was once a bustling institution, home to thousands of patients who suffered from a wide range of mental illnesses. Unfortunately, as the facility's population grew, so too did the accounts of mistreatment and abuse. Patients were subjected to cruel and inhumane treatments, including electroshock therapy, lobotomies, and even being restrained in cages. Many of the asylum's residents met their untimely deaths within its walls, leaving behind a legacy of pain, suffering, and anguish that continues to echo throughout the building.

Over the years, numerous paranormal encounters have been reported within the asylum, leading many to believe that the spirits of former patients and staff still linger in the abandoned halls. One such account comes from a visitor named Sarah, who was exploring the notorious fourth floor of the asylum, where the most violent and unstable patients were once housed. As she walked down the dimly lit corridor, she began to hear the faint sound of footsteps behind her. Turning around, she saw no one, but the sound persisted, growing louder and more frantic. Suddenly, she felt a cold, clammy hand grip her arm, leaving her frozen in terror. As quickly as the sensation had come, it vanished, leaving Sarah to ponder the presence of the restless spirits that continue to wander the asylum's halls.

Another chilling tale comes from a paranormal investigator named David, who was conducting an overnight investigation of the asylum's pharmacy. As he sat in the darkness, he began to hear the faint sound of glass bottles clinking together, as if someone was searching for something among the shelves. The sound grew louder and more persistent, until it was accompanied by the disembodied voice of a woman, softly whispering the names of various medications. David was left in awe, convinced that he had encountered the spirit of a former nurse, forever bound to her duties within the asylum's walls.

The asylum's electroshock therapy room has also been the site of numerous paranormal occurrences. During a guided tour of the facility, a group of visitors entered the room, only to be met with an overwhelming feeling of dread and unease. The air grew thick and heavy, and several members of the group claimed to see a dark, shadowy figure looming in the corner, watching them intently. As they hurried to leave the room, the door slammed shut behind them, leaving them to wonder if the spirit of a former patient was trying to communicate the terror they had experienced during their time at the asylum.

In addition to the countless personal experiences reported by those who have ventured within the Trans-Allegheny Lunatic Asylum, paranormal investigators have also captured a wealth of compelling evidence pointing to the supernatural phenomena that pervades the building. Ghostly apparitions and unexplained shadows have been caught on film, while chilling EVP recordings of disembodied voices and cries for help have been captured in the silence of the abandoned halls.

The stories and experiences of those who have explored the Trans-Allegheny Lunatic Asylum paint a vivid picture of the tortured souls that continue to haunt this once-thriving institution. The echoes of the insane reverberate through the empty corridors and abandoned rooms, serving as a constant reminder of the pain and suffering that occurred within its walls. It is said that the ghostly nurses and patients who never left the premises continue to roam the asylum, forever bound to the place where they experienced unimaginable horrors.

One particularly harrowing account comes from a group of paranormal investigators who were conducting a late-night exploration of the asylum's solitary confinement area. As they ventured deeper into the dark and oppressive space, they were overcome with a suffocating sense of despair. Suddenly, the air was filled with the sounds of sobbing and pleading, as if the spirits of the patients who had been subjected to the unbearable isolation of solitary confinement were reaching out in anguish. The investigators were left shaken, haunted by the thought of the countless souls that had been broken within the confines of the Trans-Allegheny Lunatic Asylum.

Even the grounds surrounding the asylum have not been spared from the paranormal activity that seems to permeate the entire property. A security guard named James recalls a chilling encounter he had while patrolling the perimeter of the building one foggy evening. As he walked along the edge of the property, he noticed a figure in the distance, standing near the old cemetery where many of the asylum's patients had been laid to rest. As he approached, the figure seemed to vanish into the mist, leaving no trace of its presence. James could not shake the feeling that he had witnessed the spirit of a former patient, still tethered to the asylum even in death.

The Trans-Allegheny Lunatic Asylum serves as a stark reminder of the dark and troubled history of mental health care in the United States. The suffering and anguish experienced by its patients have left an indelible mark on the building, making it a hotbed of paranormal activity and ghostly encounters. For those brave enough to venture within its haunted halls, the asylum offers a chilling glimpse into a world where the lines between the living and the dead blur, and the tortured souls of the past continue to make their presence known.

The numerous accounts of ghostly nurses, patients who never left, and the tortured souls that haunt the asylum provide a chilling testimony to the enduring power of the human spirit and its ability to transcend the boundaries of life and death. As the echoes of the insane continue to reverberate through the Trans-Allegheny Lunatic Asylum, visitors from around the world are drawn to explore its dark and foreboding halls, seeking to uncover the stories of those who suffered within and hoping to make contact with the restless spirits that linger in the shadows.

In the end, the Trans-Allegheny Lunatic Asylum stands as a monument to the countless lives that were irrevocably changed by the institution and the haunting legacy of pain, suffering, and death that still lingers within its walls. For those who dare to enter, the asylum offers a chilling and unforgettable journey into the realm of the unknown, where the echoes of the insane can still be heard, and the spirits of the tortured souls that once called the asylum home continue to roam, restless and unseen.

Old Changi Hospital

The dark history of Old Changi Hospital in Singapore is enough to send shivers down anyone's spine. Established in the 1930s as a British military hospital, this imposing facility witnessed some of the most brutal and blood-curdling events during World War II. The Japanese occupation of Singapore led to its conversion into a prison camp, where captured soldiers were subjected to heinous acts of torture and death. Since then, countless tales of restless spirits, wartime horrors, and inexplicable events have haunted the hospital grounds.

Even after the war, the hospital continued to operate, initially as a medical facility for the British military and later as a public hospital. However, its grisly past continued to cast a dark shadow over its halls. When the hospital finally closed its doors in 1997, the abandoned structure became a hotspot for paranormal enthusiasts and those seeking a chilling encounter with the supernatural.

One of the most infamous tales associated with Old Changi Hospital revolves around the spirit of a former doctor who is said to roam the corridors late at night. This Japanese doctor, known as Dr. Kempeitai, is believed to have been responsible for the brutal torture and experimentation on prisoners during the occupation. Many visitors have reported encountering a malevolent presence in the hallways, accompanied by the unnerving sound of footsteps and a sense of dread that seems to permeate the air.

A group of paranormal investigators, led by a man named Marcus, decided to spend a night at the hospital to document any supernatural occurrences. As they made their way through the dimly lit corridors, Marcus and his team felt a sudden drop in temperature, and their equipment began to malfunction inexplicably. Unnerved by the experience, the team decided to conduct a séance to communicate with the spirits that were believed to haunt the hospital.

As the séance commenced, the group witnessed a series of spine-chilling events. The candles flickered violently as a gust of cold air swept through the room, and the planchette on the Ouija board moved with purpose, spelling out the name "Kempeitai." Marcus and his team were left in shock, convinced that they had made contact with the malevolent spirit of the notorious doctor.

Another harrowing tale involves the spirit of a young girl who is believed to have died at the hospital. Many visitors have reported hearing her cries and seeing her ghostly apparition wandering the halls, searching for her mother. A woman named Linda, who had ventured into the hospital on a dare, encountered this spirit during her exploration.

As Linda navigated the dark and decaying corridors, she heard the faint sound of a child sobbing. Following the sound, she came upon a small, dishevelled girl with tears streaming down her face. Linda attempted to comfort the girl, but as she reached out to touch her, the girl vanished into thin air, leaving Linda in a state of shock and disbelief.

The numerous eyewitness accounts of supernatural encounters at Old Changi Hospital are not limited to its interior. The hospital grounds, shrouded in an eerie silence, have also been the site of several ghostly sightings. One such incident involves a group of friends who decided to explore the hospital's exterior at night. As they approached the perimeter fence, they noticed a figure standing near the entrance, dressed in what appeared to be a military uniform.

As the group drew closer, they were struck by the figure's pale, gaunt appearance, and the unnerving sensation that they were not alone. They watched as the figure seemed to dissolve into the darkness, leaving them with a chilling sense that they had come face-to-face with a spirit from the hospital's troubled past.

Despite the terrifying tales and supernatural phenomena that have come to define Old Changi Hospital, the fascination with this sinister sanctuary continues to draw visitors from all over the world. The combination of its dark history, tragic wartime events, and the numerous reports of paranormal encounters make it a chilling destination for those seeking a brush with the supernatural.

One particularly chilling story involves a group of young filmmakers who, in the hopes of capturing evidence of the paranormal, ventured into the hospital with their cameras and recording equipment. As they cautiously moved through the building, they began to pick up strange sounds on their audio recorders—whispers that seemed to carry the weight of unspeakable pain and suffering.

As the team pressed on, they entered a room that had once served as a makeshift operating theatre during the war. Here, they encountered an overwhelming feeling of despair and the unmistakable stench of decay. It was as if the air itself was saturated with the memories of the atrocities committed within those walls.

Suddenly, one of the team members felt a forceful shove from behind, causing him to stumble and fall to the ground. As he struggled to regain his footing, he noticed deep, unexplained scratches on his arms and legs. The team, now deeply unnerved, decided to abandon their investigation and hastily retreated from the hospital.

For all the terrifying stories and supernatural encounters associated with Old Changi Hospital, it remains a powerful testament to the darkest chapters of human history. The restless spirits and wartime horrors that are said to linger within its walls serve as a haunting reminder of the cruelty and suffering that transpired there.

As the tales of Old Changi Hospital continue to echo through the years, the hospital stands as a grim monument to the horrors of the past and the supernatural forces that are said to linger in its abandoned halls. Those who dare to enter its decaying confines must be prepared to confront the chilling legacy of pain and suffering that haunts this sinister sanctuary, where the weight of the past refuses to be forgotten.

Beechworth Lunatic Asylum

In the verdant hills of Victoria, Australia, a looming structure casts a dark shadow over the landscape. The Beechworth Lunatic Asylum, formerly known as Mayday Hills, stands as a chilling reminder of the tragic history of mental health treatment in the 19th and early 20th centuries. Its foreboding walls and desolate grounds harbour countless stories of suffering and despair, as well as numerous accounts of ghostly encounters and spine-chilling screams that seem to emanate from the very fabric of the building itself.

Constructed in 1867, the Beechworth Lunatic Asylum was designed to accommodate the growing number of patients in need of psychiatric care in the region. The institution was originally designed to house 1,200 patients, but at its peak, it held over 2,000, leading to overcrowding and dire living conditions. Over the 128 years of its operation, it is estimated that approximately 9,000 people died within the confines of the asylum, their souls said to linger long after their physical bodies had perished.

The treatment of patients at Beechworth Lunatic Asylum was often barbaric, reflecting the limited understanding of mental health during that era. Patients were frequently subjected to inhumane practices such as electroconvulsive therapy, isolation, and even lobotomies, as the medical community grappled with the complexities of the human mind. The asylum's grim past, combined with the overwhelming sense of despair that permeates its halls, has made it a hotbed of paranormal activity and a popular destination for those seeking encounters with the supernatural.

One of the most infamous spirits said to haunt the asylum is that of Matron Sharpe, a nurse who was known for her strict and unyielding demeanour. She ruled the wards with an iron fist, and her presence was felt long after her death. Staff and visitors alike have reported seeing her ghostly figure roaming the hallways, checking in on patients and ensuring that order is maintained. Some have even claimed to hear her footsteps echoing through the empty corridors, a chilling testament to her unrelenting dedication to her duties.

Another spirit believed to wander the grounds is that of Tommy

Kennedy, a former patient who worked as a gardener at the asylum. Tommy was a gentle soul who took solace in tending to the gardens and interacting with the other patients. His tragic death in a hit-and-run accident left a deep sense of sorrow within the institution, and many believe that his spirit remains, unable to move on. Witnesses have reported seeing his apparition in the gardens, still caring for the plants and flowers that brought him comfort in life.

A particularly chilling account comes from a group of paranormal investigators who conducted a late-night exploration of the asylum. As they made their way through the darkened hallways, they encountered a series of unexplained cold spots, accompanied by the unmistakable scent of decay. Suddenly, the oppressive silence was shattered by the sound of gut-wrenching screams, echoing through the asylum as though the anguished cries of the patients were still reverberating through the halls. Despite their best efforts to locate the source of the screams, the investigators were unable to determine their origin, leaving them with an unsettling sense of unease.

As they continued their investigation, the team ventured into the former children's ward, where the atmosphere grew even more oppressive. The air was heavy with the weight of sorrow and despair, and the investigators found it difficult to breathe. As they stood in the darkened room, they were startled by the sound of a child's laughter, quickly followed by the gentle patter of small footsteps running past them. Though they could find no trace of the child, they were left with the overwhelming sense that they were not alone in that space, and that the spirit of the young patient was still seeking solace within the confines of the asylum.

In addition to these ghostly encounters, visitors to Beechworth Lunatic Asylum have reported a wide range of paranormal phenomena, from unexplained noises and disembodied voices to sudden drops in temperature and even physical manifestations such as being touched or pushed by unseen forces. Many attribute these occurrences to the tormented souls of the patients who suffered within the asylum's walls, their spirits forever bound to the place of their anguish.

One particularly harrowing tale involves a group of tourists who embarked on a guided tour of the asylum. As they were led through the maze of corridors and rooms, they came upon the notorious Grevillea Wing, a ward reserved for the most dangerous and uncontrollable patients. As the tour guide recounted the grim history of the ward, the group suddenly heard a blood-curdling scream emanating from one of the cells. Despite their terror, they could find no logical explanation for the sound, and the tour guide later confided that she had never experienced anything like it during her time at the asylum.

The Beechworth Lunatic Asylum has also become a popular destination for ghost hunters and paranormal enthusiasts seeking to capture evidence of the supernatural on film or audio recordings. One such group conducted an extensive investigation of the asylum and managed to capture a series of eerie EVPs (electronic voice phenomena) that seemed to confirm the presence of ghostly inhabitants. Among the chilling recordings were the sounds of laboured breathing, indistinct whispers, and even the plaintive cries of a woman, believed by some to be the voice of a former patient reliving her torment in the afterlife.

Beyond the individual encounters and experiences, there is an unmistakable air of sadness and despair that permeates the grounds of the Beechworth Lunatic Asylum. Visitors often report feeling an overwhelming sense of heaviness and oppression as they explore the abandoned wards and corridors, as if the lingering remnants of the asylum's dark history continue to cast a pall over the once-thriving institution.

Today, the Beechworth Lunatic Asylum stands as a haunting reminder of the atrocities that occurred within its walls, a chilling testament to the suffering and anguish of the thousands of patients who passed through its gates. As visitors wander the halls and gaze upon the fading remnants of a bygone era, they are left to ponder the chilling tales and ghostly encounters that have come to define the asylum's legacy.

While many questions remain unanswered and the true extent of the supernatural activity at Beechworth Lunatic Asylum may never be fully understood, one thing is certain: the spirits of those who suffered within its walls continue to haunt its abandoned corridors, a chilling reminder of the dark history that lies hidden beneath the surface. As the sun sets over the hills of Victoria, casting shadows across the asylum's imposing façade, the haunting haven of Beechworth Lunatic Asylum remains a place where the lines between life and death, the natural and the supernatural, blur beyond recognition, and the restless souls of its former inhabitants continue to roam the silent halls, seeking solace in a world that has long since moved on.

Aradale Mental Hospital

Situated atop a windswept hill in Ararat, Victoria, Australia, Aradale Mental Hospital looms large, casting an ominous shadow over the surrounding landscape. Its imposing, neo-classical architecture stands as a chilling testament to the dark history that unfolded within its walls, with countless tormented souls having passed through its gates during the hospital's 130-year operation. Today, the abandoned wards of Aradale Mental Hospital are said to be haunted by the spirits of former patients and staff, their restless energy still palpable as one walks the desolate corridors.

Opened in 1867, Aradale Mental Hospital was designed by architect G.W. Vivian and was one of the largest asylums in Australia, providing care for over 2,000 patients at its peak. The hospital was established as part of a broader network of facilities intended to accommodate and treat individuals suffering from various mental illnesses. However, despite its initial mission to provide care and solace, the hospital would eventually become synonymous with suffering and cruelty.

Throughout its years of operation, Aradale Mental Hospital became notorious for its inhumane and barbaric treatment methods, which included electroconvulsive therapy, insulin coma therapy, and even lobotomies. In addition, the overcrowded and unsanitary conditions within the hospital only served to exacerbate the suffering of its patients. As a result, many lives were lost, and countless souls were left scarred by the brutal experiences they endured within the asylum's walls.

It is no wonder, then, that Aradale Mental Hospital has become a hotbed of paranormal activity and ghostly encounters, as the spirits of those who suffered and died in the facility are said to linger, unable to find peace in the afterlife. Visitors to the site have reported a wide range of chilling experiences, from disembodied voices and unexplained noises to mysterious apparitions and physical manifestations.

One such account involves a former nurse named Sarah, who worked at the hospital during its operation. According to local lore, Sarah was deeply troubled by the cruel treatments inflicted upon the patients and took her own life in the hospital's bell tower. Her spirit is said to haunt the tower to this day, with visitors reporting sightings of a ghostly figure clad in a nurse's uniform, as well as the inexplicable tolling of the bell in the dead of night.

Another unsettling tale concerns a malevolent spirit known as "The Governor," believed to be the ghost of a former staff member who was particularly cruel to the patients. Visitors have reported feeling a sinister presence in certain areas of the hospital, accompanied by a sense of dread and malice. There are even accounts of physical encounters with The Governor, with some individuals claiming to have been pushed or shoved by an unseen force.

In addition to these specific spirits, countless other ghostly encounters have been reported throughout Aradale Mental Hospital. From the unnerving laughter of unseen children echoing through the wards to the anguished cries of former patients reverberating in the corridors, the asylum seems to be a repository for the psychic energy of its tragic past.

One particularly compelling account comes from a group of paranormal investigators who visited the hospital in search of evidence of the supernatural. During their investigation, they captured a series of eerie EVPs (electronic voice phenomena) that appeared to confirm the presence of otherworldly entities within the hospital. Among the chilling recordings were the sounds of laboured breathing, indistinct whispers, and even the plaintive cries of a woman, believed by some to be the voice of a former patient reliving her torment in the afterlife.

Beyond these individual accounts, Aradale Mental Hospital has also become the site of organised ghost tours, allowing visitors the opportunity to explore the abandoned wards and haunted corridors firsthand. These tours have resulted in numerous additional accounts of paranormal experiences, with guests reporting everything from cold spots and inexplicable temperature fluctuations to feelings of being watched and even touched by unseen hands.

One such tour participant, a woman named Emily, recalled an unnerving experience in the hospital's infamous ECT (electroconvulsive therapy) room. As she entered the dimly lit space, she felt a sudden, overwhelming sense of sadness and despair. Moments later, she reported feeling an icy cold hand gently caressing her cheek, as if to offer comfort. Emily believes that she was in the presence of a spirit – perhaps that of a former patient who had endured the horrors of ECT and sought to share their pain with her.

Another tour-goer, James, shared a chilling encounter in one of the hospital's isolation cells. As he stood in the small, windowless room, he was overcome by a suffocating sense of claustrophobia and panic. Suddenly, he felt a sharp tug on the back of his shirt, as if someone was trying to pull him out of the room. Upon exiting the cell, James was certain that he had been in the presence of a tormented spirit who had been confined to the cell during their time at the hospital.

It is not only the spirits of former patients that are said to haunt the abandoned halls of Aradale Mental Hospital, but also those of the staff who worked there. One tour guide, Laura, shared a particularly poignant encounter with a spirit she believes was a former nurse at the hospital. While leading a group through the wards, Laura noticed a woman dressed in period clothing standing in a doorway, watching her with a solemn expression. When Laura attempted to approach the woman, she vanished without a trace. Laura later discovered that the nurse's uniform the spirit was wearing matched those worn by the hospital's staff during the early 1900s, leading her to believe that the spirit was that of a former nurse, perhaps still watching over her patients in the afterlife.

As the sun sets over the desolate grounds of Aradale Mental

Hospital, the shadows grow long, and the chilling echoes of its dark history come to life once more. The spirits of those who once sought solace and healing within its walls continue to roam the abandoned wards, their voices and stories still resonating in the eerie silence. For those who dare to venture into the unsettling halls of madness, Aradale Mental Hospital serves as a chilling reminder of the suffering that unfolded within its walls and the restless spirits who continue to haunt its corridors to this day.

Taunton State Hospital

Located in Taunton, Massachusetts, Taunton State Hospital was once a thriving psychiatric institution, built in 1854 to provide care and treatment for the mentally ill. Over the years, however, the hospital's history became marred by tales of abuse, neglect, and suffering. As the facility declined and eventually closed its doors in 1975, it left behind a legacy of pain and anguish that continues to echo through its abandoned halls. Today, Taunton State Hospital is widely regarded as one of the most haunted locations in Massachusetts, with countless stories of ghostly patients and shadowy figures roaming its desolate corridors.

One of the most chilling aspects of Taunton State Hospital's history is the so-called "Underground Tunnel System." This series of tunnels connected the various buildings of the hospital complex, allowing staff and patients to move between them without having to venture outside. While these tunnels were originally intended for practical purposes, they soon became the site of numerous unsettling incidents and paranormal encounters. Visitors to the hospital have reported feeling a sense of dread and unease as they ventured into the dimly lit tunnels, with some claiming to have witnessed shadowy figures lurking in the darkness.

One such encounter occurred when a group of urban explorers decided to brave the tunnels for themselves. As they ventured deeper into the system, they began to hear faint whispers echoing through the darkness, as if someone or something was attempting to communicate with them. The whispers grew louder and more insistent, ultimately culminating in a blood-curdling scream that sent the group fleeing in terror. To this day, the identity of the voice remains a mystery, but many speculate that it belonged to a former patient who had been subjected to the hospital's inhumane treatments and continued to haunt the tunnels in search of solace.

The main hospital building itself is no stranger to paranormal activity. Over the years, numerous visitors have reported encounters with ghostly patients and staff members who seem to have never left the facility. One such visitor, a man named Mark, was exploring the hospital with a group of friends when he became separated from the others. As he wandered the darkened halls alone, he suddenly came face to face with a woman in a tattered, bloodstained hospital gown. The woman appeared to be in great distress and reached out to him, her eyes filled with tears. Before Mark could react, the woman vanished into thin air, leaving him shaken and bewildered.

In addition to the ghostly patients, many visitors to Taunton State Hospital have reported encounters with a mysterious entity known as the "Creeper." This shadowy figure is said to crawl along the floors, walls, and ceilings of the hospital, often appearing in the peripheral vision of those who venture into the building. The Creeper is believed to be a malevolent spirit, feeding off the negative energy that permeates the hospital's abandoned wards. Those who have encountered the Creeper describe an overwhelming sense of fear and dread, with some claiming to have been physically touched or scratched by the entity.

One particularly harrowing account of the Creeper comes from a paranormal investigator named Sarah, who visited the hospital with her team in hopes of documenting evidence of the supernatural. As they made their way through the building, Sarah suddenly felt a presence looming over her, and when she looked up, she was confronted by the sight of a dark figure clinging to the ceiling above her. The figure quickly disappeared, but not before leaving deep scratches on Sarah's arm, as if attempting to mark her as its own.

While the ghostly patients and the Creeper may be the most well-known entities said to haunt Taunton State Hospital, there are many other spirits that visitors have claimed to encounter within its walls.

Within the grounds of the hospital, there is a small, overgrown cemetery that serves as the final resting place for many former patients. The cemetery, once a peaceful and solemn space, has now become the site of numerous ghostly sightings and paranormal occurrences. Visitors have reported seeing apparitions wandering among the tombstones, seemingly unaware of their own passing. Disembodied voices and unexplained sounds are also a common occurrence in the cemetery, with some claiming to have heard the cries and whispers of the restless spirits who remain trapped within the confines of the hospital grounds.

One of the most chilling tales associated with the cemetery is that of a young boy named David, who was committed to the hospital in the early 1900s. Suffering from an unknown mental illness, David was subjected to a series of experimental treatments that ultimately led to his untimely death. It is said that his spirit now roams the cemetery, searching for the family he was taken from so many years ago. Visitors to the cemetery have reported encountering David's ghost, describing him as a sad and lonely figure who seems to be searching for something or someone he can never find.

The haunting stories of Taunton State Hospital are not limited to its patients and staff. Some visitors have reported encountering the spirits of former caretakers and even doctors who once worked within the facility. One such doctor, Dr. Martin, is said to have been a particularly cruel and heartless individual who subjected his patients to torturous treatments in the name of science. After his death, it is believed that Dr. Martin's spirit became trapped within the hospital, condemned to roam its halls for all eternity. Visitors have reported seeing his ghostly figure wandering the facility, still dressed in his white lab coat and carrying a clipboard, as if he is still conducting his twisted experiments on the unfortunate souls who remain imprisoned within the hospital walls.

As the years have passed and the stories of Taunton State Hospital have continued to grow, the facility has become a popular destination for ghost hunters, urban explorers, and paranormal enthusiasts. Many have ventured into the decaying halls of the hospital, hoping to catch a glimpse of the spirits that are said to haunt its grounds. Some have left with chilling tales of their own, while others have been left with nothing more than a sense of unease and a lingering feeling of sorrow for the lost souls who continue to inhabit the hospital.

In recent years, efforts have been made to preserve the history of Taunton State Hospital and to ensure that the stories of its patients and staff are not forgotten. The hospital complex has been added to the National Register of Historic Places, and there are ongoing discussions about potential redevelopment or repurposing of the site. For now, however, Taunton State Hospital remains an eerie and abandoned monument to the darker side of psychiatric care and a haunting reminder of the suffering and anguish that once filled its halls.

As you journey through the pages of this book and explore the chilling tales of haunted hospitals and asylums around the world, remember the lost souls of Taunton State Hospital. Their stories serve as a sobering reminder of the pain and suffering that can occur within the walls of medical institutions and as a testament to the resilience of the human spirit, which continues to linger even in the face of unimaginable hardship and despair.

Poveglia Island

The Venetian Lagoon, a vast expanse of water in northeastern Italy, is home to more than a hundred islands, some inhabited, others abandoned. Among these islands lies the chilling and forsaken Poveglia Island, a place that has borne witness to unspeakable horrors throughout its history. Poveglia Island has been shrouded in an eerie atmosphere, haunted by the tormented souls of plague victims and other unfortunate souls who once inhabited its decaying hospital buildings.

The island's dark history dates back to the 14th century when the bubonic plague ravaged Europe. As the death toll mounted, the Venetian authorities designated Poveglia as a quarantine site, where the infected would be isolated to prevent the spread of the deadly disease. Over the centuries, thousands of plague victims were brought to the island, where they lived out their final days in agony and despair. The island's soil is said to be mixed with the ashes of countless human remains, a grim reminder of the suffering that took place on its shores.

As if the island's macabre past were not enough, in the 19th century, a mental asylum was constructed on Poveglia Island. The facility was intended to provide care and treatment for the mentally ill, but instead, it became a place of torment and abuse. Rumours circulated of patients being subjected to cruel and inhumane experiments at the hands of the staff, and the asylum's chief doctor was said to be a sadistic and twisted man who took pleasure in his patients' pain.

The asylum was eventually closed in the mid-20th century, and Poveglia Island was left abandoned, with its decaying structures and horrifying history as its only legacy. Today, the island is off-limits to the general public, but the tales of its haunted past continue to intrigue and horrify those who dare to explore its chilling secrets.

Visitors who have managed to set foot on the island have reported a wide array of paranormal phenomena. Disembodied voices, eerie footsteps, and chilling screams are often heard echoing through the empty corridors of the former hospital buildings. The spirits of plague victims and asylum patients are said to wander the island, trapped in a never-ending cycle of suffering and anguish. The air on the island is thick with an overwhelming sense of dread and despair, a feeling that is impossible to shake off.

One of the most famous ghosts said to haunt Poveglia Island is the malevolent spirit of the asylum's chief doctor. According to legend, the doctor performed gruesome and unspeakable experiments on his patients, often causing more harm than good. His cruelty and madness eventually led to his own demise, as he reportedly threw himself from the bell tower of the asylum, driven to suicide by the tortured souls of his patients. His ghost is said to still haunt the island, lurking in the shadows, forever bound to the site of his horrific deeds.

The spirits of plague victims are also said to roam the island, their anguished cries and moans echoing through the night. Many visitors have reported encountering these tormented souls, their spectral forms appearing suddenly and then vanishing just as quickly, leaving behind an oppressive feeling of sadness and grief. The island's atmosphere is permeated by a profound sense of loss and pain, as if the very ground itself is crying out in anguish.

The island is also home to a number of lesser-known spirits, each with their own tragic stories to tell. One such spirit is that of a young girl named Isabella, who was mistakenly brought to the island during the plague and left to die alongside the infected. Her ghost is said to haunt the island's shores, searching in vain for a way to escape the island and return to her family. Visitors have reported seeing her tearful apparition, dressed in tattered clothing, as she wanders along the water's edge, her cries for help carried away by the wind.

Another tragic figure said to roam Poveglia Island is a former nurse from the mental asylum, who is believed to have taken her own life after witnessing the horrors inflicted upon the patients in her care. Her ghost has been seen wandering the empty halls of the asylum, her footsteps echoing softly in the darkness. The sorrowful spirit is said to be trapped on the island, unable to find peace or forgiveness for her role in the patients' suffering.

In addition to the many ghostly sightings, visitors to Poveglia Island have reported experiencing a wide array of inexplicable and unsettling phenomena. Some have described feeling an intense pressure on their chest, as if the air itself were trying to suffocate them, while others have reported being overcome with sudden waves of nausea and dizziness. Unexplained cold spots and fluctuations in temperature have also been documented, as well as instances of electronic equipment failing without reason.

The haunting tales and supernatural occurrences on Poveglia Island have attracted the attention of paranormal investigators from around the world, eager to uncover the truth behind the island's ghostly inhabitants. One such investigation was conducted by the popular television show "Ghost Adventures," which featured the island in a 2009 episode. During their visit, the crew encountered a number of unexplained events, including disembodied voices, strange sounds, and the feeling of being touched by unseen hands. Their experiences on the island only served to further cement Poveglia's reputation as one of the most haunted places on earth.

Despite the numerous accounts of paranormal activity and the chilling history that pervades the island, the Italian government has recently considered reopening Poveglia to the public. In an effort to raise funds for the restoration and preservation of the island's historic structures, proposals have been made to transform the island into a luxury hotel or museum. However, the idea of redeveloping the island has been met with fierce opposition from those who believe that Poveglia's tragic past should remain undisturbed.

The chilling tales and supernatural encounters that surround Poveglia Island serve as a harrowing reminder of the suffering and torment that took place on its shores. As one of Italy's most haunted locations, the island continues to draw the curious and the brave, those who seek to unravel the mysteries that lie beneath the surface of this forsaken place.

Whether Poveglia's future lies in redevelopment or continued abandonment, one thing remains certain: the spirits of the tormented souls who once inhabited the island will continue to haunt its decaying hospital buildings, trapped in a world of pain and sorrow, their cries echoing through the night, a testament to the island's dark and tragic past.

Severalls Hospital

In the verdant countryside of Essex, England, the imposing ruins of Severalls Hospital stand as a chilling reminder of the suffering and torment experienced within its walls. This notorious psychiatric hospital, which operated from 1913 to 1997, once housed thousands of mentally ill patients, many of whom endured controversial and inhumane treatments. Today, the decaying remains of the hospital serve as a haunting testament to the dark history of mental healthcare in the early 20th century, and the building is reputed to be inhabited by the restless spirits of those who suffered there.

Constructed on a sprawling 300-acre site, Severalls Hospital was designed to accommodate up to 2,000 patients and was one of the largest psychiatric facilities in the country. The asylum was self-sufficient, with its own power plant, water supply, and even a railway that connected it to the nearby town of Colchester. The sprawling complex of red brick buildings was connected by a series of covered walkways, allowing staff and patients to move between the wards without being exposed to the elements.

During its operation, Severalls Hospital bore witness to a multitude of controversial and brutal treatments, including lobotomies, electroconvulsive therapy, and the administration of powerful drugs. Many patients were subjected to these procedures against their will, and some even experienced multiple surgeries in an attempt to cure their mental illnesses. The questionable ethics of these treatments, combined with the often overcrowded and unsanitary conditions, contributed to the suffering of countless patients who passed through the hospital's doors.

With such a dark and turbulent history, it is little wonder that the abandoned halls of Severalls Hospital are said to be haunted by the spirits of those who endured unimaginable pain and suffering within its walls. Over the years, numerous witnesses have reported chilling encounters and supernatural phenomena, ranging from disembodied voices and unexplained footsteps to the apparitions of former patients and staff members.

One of the most infamous ghostly residents of Severalls Hospital is that of a young woman named Mary, who is believed to have been a patient at the asylum during the early 20th century.

According to local legend, Mary suffered from severe mental illness and was subjected to multiple lobotomies in a futile attempt to alleviate her symptoms. The repeated surgeries left her disfigured and unable to speak, and she spent the remainder of her days confined to the hospital. Witnesses have reported encountering Mary's spirit in the abandoned wards, where her anguished cries echo through the empty corridors, a chilling reminder of the torment she endured during her time at Severalls.

Another well-known ghostly inhabitant of the hospital is that of a former nurse, known as Nurse Collins. Rumoured to have worked at the hospital during the 1950s, she was known for her strict and sometimes cruel demeanour. According to accounts, Nurse Collins was particularly fond of humiliating her patients and would often punish them with physical force. Today, her spirit is said to roam the now-abandoned corridors, still clad in her old-fashioned nursing uniform. Many who have ventured into the hospital claim to have heard the sound of her footsteps echoing through the halls, and some even report being shoved or struck by an unseen force, as if Nurse Collins were still meting out her cruel punishments.

In addition to these ghostly inhabitants, visitors to Severalls

Hospital have experienced a wide range of inexplicable phenomena. Unexplained noises, such as banging doors, slamming windows, and whispered voices, have been frequently reported, as well as sudden drops in temperature and the sensation of being watched. In the hospital's chapel, a sinister presence is said to lurk, and some visitors claim to have been overcome with an overwhelming feeling of dread upon entering the room.

In the disused operating theatre, witnesses have reported encountering the apparition of a surgeon, still dressed in his bloodstained scrubs. This spectral figure is said to be particularly active at night, with many visitors claiming to have seen him standing over a phantom operating table, seemingly performing surgery on an unseen patient. The sounds of medical equipment and the cries of the patient have also been reported, creating a chilling atmosphere that leaves even the most sceptical visitor shaken.

One particularly harrowing account comes from a group of urban explorers who ventured into the hospital in search of the paranormal. As they made their way through the decaying wards, they came across a room filled with dusty old wheelchairs. Intrigued, they began to take photographs, hoping to capture evidence of the hospital's ghostly inhabitants. Suddenly, they heard the sound of a wheelchair being moved, followed by the distinct sound of footsteps approaching them. The group, gripped with terror, fled the room, only to later discover a photograph they had taken of a shadowy figure seated in one of the wheelchairs.

Another unnerving experience comes from a paranormal investigator who spent a night inside Severalls Hospital in an attempt to document the supernatural occurrences. As he sat in the pitch-black darkness of a former patient's room, he suddenly heard the sound of a child's laughter coming from the hallway outside. Upon investigating, he discovered a small ball rolling down the corridor, as if pushed by an unseen hand. As he reached out to pick up the ball, it suddenly shot away from him, propelled by an unseen force, and the sound of laughter echoed through the empty halls.

The haunting tales of Severalls Hospital serve as a stark reminder of the suffering and torment experienced within its walls. Today, the decaying ruins stand as a testament to the dark history of mental healthcare and the spirits that are believed to linger there. As more people are drawn to explore the chilling remains of the hospital, the stories of ghostly encounters and supernatural phenomena continue to grow. Whether driven by a desire to experience the paranormal or simply to bear witness to the eerie remnants of a bygone era, those who venture into Severalls Hospital are sure to leave with a sense of unease, and perhaps even a chilling encounter with one of its ghostly inhabitants.

Gonjiam Psychiatric Hospital

Once a place of refuge and healing for the mentally ill, the Gonjiam Psychiatric Hospital in Gyeonggi-do, South Korea, now stands as a chilling reminder of the suffering and torment experienced by its patients. Abandoned for decades, the hospital has earned a reputation as one of the most haunted places in South Korea, with countless tales of ghostly encounters and unexplained phenomena swirling around its decaying halls.

The history of Gonjiam Psychiatric Hospital is shrouded in mystery, with little known about the facility's past. It is said to have been built in the 1960s, and during its operation, the hospital housed patients suffering from a range of psychiatric disorders. However, rumours began to circulate that the hospital's owner was engaging in unethical practices, leading to the suffering and even death of numerous patients. Eventually, the facility was closed down in the 1990s, leaving the building to rot and decay.

Over time, the abandoned hospital began to attract thrill-seekers and paranormal enthusiasts, all eager to catch a glimpse of the supernatural phenomena said to occur within its walls. Some visitors have claimed to have seen the spirits of former patients, still dressed in their hospital gowns, wandering the dark and dusty corridors. Others have reported hearing the distant cries and screams of those who once resided in the facility, echoing through the empty rooms.

One harrowing account comes from a group of friends who decided to venture into the hospital in search of the paranormal. As they made their way through the dark, crumbling hallways, they suddenly heard the sound of footsteps behind them. As they turned to investigate, they were horrified to see a ghostly figure dressed in a white hospital gown, with hollow eyes and a twisted expression of pain and anguish. The apparition appeared to be following them, only to vanish when they tried to approach it.

Another spine-chilling tale comes from a paranormal investigator who spent a night alone in the hospital, determined to document any evidence of supernatural activity. As he sat in one of the abandoned patient rooms, he began to hear faint whispers coming from the hallway. As he ventured out to investigate, he was startled by the sudden sound of a door slamming shut behind him. As he turned to leave, he found that the door had been mysteriously locked, trapping him inside the eerie confines of the hospital.

In addition to the ghostly patients said to roam the halls, many visitors to Gonjiam Psychiatric Hospital have also reported experiencing strange and unsettling sensations. Some have described feeling a sudden drop in temperature or an oppressive sense of dread, as though they were being watched by unseen eyes. Others have reported that their electronic devices, such as cameras and cell phones, have malfunctioned or lost power without explanation.

One particularly chilling encounter comes from a group of amateur ghost hunters who ventured into the hospital at night, armed with only flashlights and a video camera. As they made their way through the darkened corridors, they began to hear strange noises coming from one of the patient rooms. As they cautiously entered the room, they were horrified to discover the walls covered in what appeared to be bloodstains. As they continued to explore the room, they suddenly heard the sound of laboured breathing, as though someone was gasping for air. Panicked, they fled the room, only to find that the bloodstains had mysteriously vanished when they later returned to investigate.

Despite the countless stories of ghostly encounters and supernatural phenomena, the true history of Gonjiam Psychiatric Hospital remains shrouded in mystery. Some speculate that the hospital's tragic past has left an indelible mark on the building, causing the spirits of those who suffered there to linger in its forsaken halls. Others believe that the building itself has absorbed the pain and anguish of its former patients, transforming it into a hotbed of paranormal activity.

In recent years, the abandoned hospital has gained international notoriety, thanks in part to the 2018 South Korean horror film "Gonjiam: Haunted Asylum," which was inspired by the real-life hospital and its chilling reputation. Since the release of the film, the site has attracted even more visitors, eager to explore the dark and foreboding building for themselves.

One group of curious explorers managed to capture what they believe to be evidence of the supernatural within the hospital walls. As they recorded their journey through the decaying building, they stumbled upon an old wheelchair, seemingly abandoned in the middle of a hallway. As they approached, they were shocked to see the wheelchair begin to move on its own, as though pushed by an invisible force. Startled, they quickly left the area, unsure of what they had just witnessed.

The fascination with Gonjiam Psychiatric Hospital shows no signs of waning, as more and more people are drawn to explore its shadowy halls and unravel the mysteries that lie within. Whether driven by a desire for an adrenaline-fueled adventure or a genuine interest in the paranormal, those who dare to enter the abandoned hospital are left with chilling tales of ghostly encounters and inexplicable events that defy rational explanation.

As the sun sets and darkness falls upon the desolate grounds of Gonjiam Psychiatric Hospital, the once-bustling facility takes on an eerie, otherworldly quality. The echoing cries of former patients and the restless spirits that are said to roam its halls serve as a haunting reminder of the suffering that once took place within its walls.

St. Albans Sanatorium

The state of Virginia, known for its lush landscapes and rich history, is home to a haunting presence in the form of St. Albans Sanatorium. This once-thriving medical facility, situated in the picturesque rolling hills of southwestern Virginia, has transformed into a hub of paranormal activity and ghostly encounters. As we delve into the unsettling past of St. Albans, we will uncover the chilling stories and unexplained phenomena that continue to mystify those who dare to explore its abandoned halls.

St. Albans was originally built as a boys' preparatory school in 1892, founded by Dr. John C. King. However, the peaceful tranquility of this educational institution was short-lived, as the school soon gained a reputation for violent incidents and a high rate of student suicides. As these tragic events accumulated, the school closed its doors in 1904, paving the way for its transformation into a state-of-the-art sanatorium in 1916.

Under the guidance of Dr. John C. Coleman, St. Albans Sanatorium focused on the treatment of mental health disorders, with a particular emphasis on hydrotherapy and electroconvulsive therapy. The facility expanded rapidly, reaching its peak in the 1950s, when it was widely regarded as one of the most advanced mental health institutions in the United States. However, with the advent of modern psychiatric medications and treatment methods, the sanatorium began to decline in the latter half of the 20th century, eventually closing its doors for good in 1992.

As the building lay abandoned and decaying, stories of ghostly encounters and unexplained phenomena began to emerge, drawing the attention of paranormal investigators and thrill-seekers alike. The sanatorium's tragic past, marked by violence and suffering, is believed to have left an indelible imprint on the very fabric of the building, with the restless spirits of former patients and staff said to linger in its forsaken halls.

One of the most frequently reported sightings at St. Albans is the apparition of a woman believed to be a former nurse named Gina. Witnesses have described encountering her ghostly form in the sanatorium's old hydrotherapy room, where she appears to be eternally tending to the needs of her long-gone patients. The spirit of Gina is often described as a friendly presence, offering comfort and solace to those who venture into the eerie depths of the sanatorium.

In stark contrast to the gentle spirit of Gina, the malevolent presence of a former patient known as Jacob has been reported by numerous visitors to St. Albans. Jacob, a tormented soul with a history of violence, is said to stalk the corridors of the sanatorium's lower levels, where he is believed to have been confined during his time as a patient. Those who have encountered Jacob's spirit have reported feelings of overwhelming dread and fear, with some even claiming to have been physically assaulted by the malevolent entity.

The ghostly figure of a little girl named Emily is another well-known inhabitant of St. Albans. Emily is often seen playing in the abandoned hallways and rooms of the sanatorium, her laughter echoing through the desolate spaces. Many visitors have reported hearing the sound of a bouncing ball, only to discover the apparition of Emily chasing after it, her playful spirit undiminished by the passage of time.

In addition to these resident spirits, countless visitors to St. Albans have reported experiencing unexplained phenomena that defy rational explanation. Disembodied voices and whispers have been heard echoing through the empty corridors, while ghostly footsteps seem to follow in the wake of those who dare to explore the dark recesses of the sanatorium. Cold spots, sudden temperature drops, and inexplicable shifts in the atmosphere are frequently encountered within the walls of St. Albans, leaving visitors with an overwhelming sense of unease and the feeling of being watched by unseen eyes.

A particularly chilling account comes from a group of paranormal investigators who ventured into the sanatorium's infamous electroconvulsive therapy room. As they stood among the decaying remnants of the once-advanced medical equipment, the team reported hearing the agonising screams of unseen patients, as if they were reliving the terrifying experiences of the past. The intense emotional energy that filled the room was so overwhelming that several members of the team were brought to tears, unable to shake the feeling of despair and torment that seemed to permeate the very air around them.

Another harrowing tale comes from a visitor who found herself inexplicably drawn to the sanatorium's former morgue. As she stepped into the cold, sterile room, she was overcome with a sense of dread and foreboding. As she turned to leave, she claims to have seen a ghostly figure lying on one of the morgue's metal slabs, the apparition's hollow eyes staring back at her with a mixture of sadness and accusation. The encounter left the visitor shaken to her core, unable to forget the haunted gaze of the spirit that seemed to beg for release from its eternal torment.

The ghostly encounters and unexplained phenomena that continue to plague St. Albans Sanatorium have transformed this once-revered institution of healing into a chilling portal to the paranormal. As visitors and investigators alike continue to be drawn to its decaying halls, they are left with no doubt that the tragic history of St. Albans has left an indelible mark on the building and its inhabitants, both seen and unseen.

As we emerge from our exploration of the haunted halls of St. Albans Sanatorium, we are left with a greater understanding of the deep connection between the living and the dead, as well as the enduring impact of human suffering on the world around us. The restless spirits that continue to roam the forsaken corridors of this once-great medical facility serve as a stark reminder of the darker side of our collective past, and the haunting legacy of pain and anguish that can linger long after our earthly existence has come to an end.

Whether you choose to believe in the supernatural or remain sceptical of the ghostly encounters and unexplained phenomena that have come to define St. Albans Sanatorium, there is no denying the chilling aura that permeates the very walls of this historic building. As the stories of ghostly inhabitants and paranormal activity continue to accumulate, St. Albans Sanatorium will remain an enduring testament to the power of the human spirit and the enduring mystery of the unknown.

Pennhurst Asylum

The tragic history and reported hauntings of this infamous state school and mental hospital have captivated the imaginations of ghost hunters, paranormal enthusiasts, and history buffs alike. Located in Spring City, Pennsylvania, Pennhurst Asylum first opened its doors in 1908, under the original name "Eastern Pennsylvania State Institution for the Feeble-Minded and Epileptic." Throughout its 79-year history, the facility housed thousands of patients, many of whom were subjected to cruel and inhumane treatments that have left a lasting impact on the very walls of this haunting institution.

Pennhurst Asylum was initially designed to offer care and support to individuals with physical and mental disabilities. However, over time, it became a dumping ground for society's unwanted, including the homeless, orphans, and even criminals. This overcrowding and lack of proper resources led to a rapid decline in the quality of care, with patients often suffering from neglect, abuse, and unsanitary living conditions.

As the years went on, the horrors that unfolded within the walls of Pennhurst Asylum became widely known, thanks to a series of exposés and investigations that ultimately led to its closure in 1987. Since then, the abandoned buildings have been left to decay, their once-bustling halls now silent and forsaken. Yet, while the living have long since abandoned Pennhurst Asylum, the spirits of those who suffered within its confines are said to remain, their restless energy permeating the eerie atmosphere of this haunted institution.

Many visitors to the asylum have reported a wide variety of paranormal activity, from disembodied voices and unexplained footsteps to full-bodied apparitions and physical contact with unseen entities. These ghostly encounters serve as a chilling reminder of the suffering and torment that once took place within the walls of Pennhurst Asylum, where the echoes of the past continue to reverberate through its haunted halls.

One particularly chilling account comes from a group of paranormal investigators who ventured into the crumbling buildings of Pennhurst in search of evidence of the supernatural. As they made their way through the darkened hallways, the team reported hearing disembodied voices, crying out in anguish and despair. The chilling sounds seemed to emanate from all around them, as if the spirits of the former patients were trying to make their presence known.

In another harrowing tale, a visitor exploring the grounds of the asylum claims to have witnessed a ghostly apparition of a young girl, her eyes filled with sadness and fear. As the visitor approached the spirit, it vanished before their eyes, leaving behind a heavy sense of sorrow and heartache. This encounter is just one of many that have been reported at Pennhurst Asylum, where the restless spirits of the past seem to be trapped within the confines of the now-abandoned institution.

Some visitors to Pennhurst Asylum have reported experiencing physical contact with unseen entities, such as being touched, pushed, or even scratched by an invisible force. These chilling encounters often occur in the more isolated areas of the asylum, where the spirits are said to be most active. Many believe that these aggressive encounters are a manifestation of the anger and frustration felt by the former patients, whose suffering and torment were left unanswered in life.

Another eerie phenomenon that has been reported at Pennhurst Asylum is the appearance of unexplained shadows and dark figures that seem to lurk in the periphery of one's vision. These mysterious entities, often referred to as "shadow people," have been known to dart in and out of the darkness, seemingly watching the living from a distance. Some visitors have even claimed to see the shadowy figures standing over them as they sleep, their chilling presence serving as a haunting reminder of the asylum's tragic past.

In addition to the ghostly encounters and unexplained phenomena experienced by visitors, the haunted history of Pennhurst Asylum has also been documented through a variety of investigative techniques, such as EVP (Electronic Voice Phenomenon) recordings and ghostly photography. These methods have captured evidence of the supernatural, further solidifying the belief that the spirits of the asylum's former patients and staff continue to linger within its crumbling walls.

In one notable EVP recording, the voice of a woman can be heard whispering a cryptic message, seemingly reaching out from beyond the grave. Some paranormal researchers believe that this voice belongs to a former nurse who once worked at Pennhurst, her spirit still wandering the halls of the asylum, trying to care for the patients who are no longer there.

Photographic evidence of the supernatural at Pennhurst Asylum includes images of ghostly apparitions, unexplained orbs of light, and even mysterious mists that appear to envelop the decaying buildings. These chilling photographs serve as further proof of the paranormal activity that is said to permeate the atmosphere of this haunted institution.

As the years pass and the memories of Pennhurst Asylum fade, the spirits that are believed to haunt its abandoned halls continue to bear witness to the suffering and torment that once took place within its confines. Despite the passage of time and the encroachment of nature upon the crumbling buildings, the echoes of the past remain, as if the very walls of the asylum have absorbed the pain and anguish of its former inhabitants.

For those who dare to venture into the haunted halls of Pennhurst Asylum, the experience is one that is both chilling and awe-inspiring, as they come face to face with the spirits of the past and the remnants of a once-thriving institution. The tragic history and reported hauntings of this infamous state school and mental hospital serve as a stark reminder of the dark side of humanity, where suffering and cruelty were allowed to fester unchecked.

As the stories and eyewitness accounts of Pennhurst Asylum's paranormal activity continue to accumulate, it becomes increasingly clear that this haunted institution stands as a testament to the resilience of the human spirit, even in the face of unimaginable suffering. For those who have experienced the chilling presence of the asylum's ghostly inhabitants, there is no doubt that the restless spirits of the past continue to roam the abandoned halls of Pennhurst, seeking solace and a chance to be heard, even in death.

So, as we immerse ourselves in the eerie, hallowed halls of institutions like Pennhurst Asylum, we must remember the tragic histories and chilling tales that have transformed these once-revered medical facilities into harbingers of the supernatural, where ghostly apparitions and inexplicable occurrences have become the norm. As we delve deep into the world of the unknown, where the spirits of those who once sought healing and solace continue to roam, restless and unseen, we are reminded of the thin line that separates life from death and the everlasting impact that our actions can have on those who are no longer with us.

Royal Hope Hospital

Situated in the sunshine state, Florida's Royal Hope Hospital has earned its place among the most chilling haunted hospitals in the world. Once a bustling military hospital, the now-abandoned building is believed to be haunted by the restless spirits of former patients and staff, who continue to wander its desolate halls.

The Royal Hope Hospital dates back to the early 1900s when it was constructed as a medical facility to serve the needs of military personnel and their families. Throughout its years of operation, the hospital treated countless soldiers and civilians for a wide range of ailments and injuries. However, its history is marred by tales of tragedy and suffering, with whispers of unethical medical practices and negligence haunting the institution's past.

As time wore on and the hospital's reputation suffered, Royal Hope Hospital eventually closed its doors, leaving behind an eerie, abandoned shell. It is within these empty halls that countless witnesses have reported experiencing unexplained phenomena and ghostly encounters, solidifying the hospital's status as a paranormal hotspot.

One of the most famous ghostly residents of Royal Hope Hospital is said to be a spectral nurse, whose apparition has been seen by numerous visitors to the abandoned facility. Clad in a vintage nurse's uniform, she is often spotted roaming the hallways, as if still tending to her patients. Those who have encountered this phantom nurse describe feeling an overwhelming sense of sorrow and compassion emanating from her presence, as though she continues to mourn the suffering that occurred within the hospital's walls.

In addition to the ghostly nurse, many visitors have also reported encounters with wandering spirits throughout the hospital. Some describe seeing shadowy figures darting around corners or disappearing into thin air, while others have heard the faint sounds of footsteps and hushed voices echoing through the empty corridors.

One particularly chilling account comes from a group of urban explorers who ventured into the hospital's long-abandoned basement. As they navigated the dark, damp space, they suddenly heard the unmistakable sound of a woman sobbing in the distance. Following the heart-wrenching cries, they stumbled upon a small room, where the sobbing abruptly stopped. Despite their thorough search of the area, the source of the cries was never found, leaving the explorers with the unnerving feeling that they had been led there by a supernatural presence.

Another eerie incident occurred during a paranormal investigation at Royal Hope Hospital, when a team of investigators attempted to make contact with the spirits said to haunt the facility. Armed with a variety of equipment, including digital voice recorders and electromagnetic field detectors, the team set out to document any evidence of paranormal activity.

As they explored the hospital's abandoned operating rooms, the investigators were startled by the sudden appearance of a ghostly figure, standing silently in the corner of the room. The apparition, which appeared to be a male patient in a hospital gown, stared at the investigators with an expression of anguish before vanishing before their eyes. Although shaken by the encounter, the investigators later discovered an EVP recording captured during the incident, which revealed the faint sound of a man's voice pleading for help.

In addition to the various eyewitness accounts, many visitors to Royal Hope Hospital have also reported experiencing a wide range of inexplicable phenomena. Some have felt sudden cold spots in the middle of the warm Florida climate, while others have been overcome by a sense of dread or sadness that lifts as soon as they leave the premises.

Still, others have reported experiencing strange physical sensations, such as being touched or brushed against by unseen hands. One woman even claimed that she was momentarily paralyzed by an unseen force while exploring the hospital's empty wards, unable to move until she begged the spirits to release her.

Despite the numerous accounts of ghostly encounters and supernatural phenomena at Royal Hope Hospital, sceptics argue that these experiences can be attributed to the power of suggestion or the natural human tendency to see patterns and assign meaning to random events. They contend that the hospital's eerie atmosphere and tragic past can easily lead visitors to interpret ordinary occurrences as paranormal in nature.

However, those who have experienced the unexplained

phenomena at Royal Hope Hospital firsthand maintain that there is more to these encounters than mere coincidence or imagination. They argue that the hospital's troubled history and the lingering energy of the suffering that took place within its walls have created a breeding ground for restless spirits and supernatural activity.

Regardless of whether one is a believer or sceptic, it is undeniable that the stories surrounding Royal Hope Hospital have captured the imagination of countless individuals. The hospital's chilling past and the numerous accounts of ghostly encounters continue to draw visitors and paranormal investigators alike, each seeking to unravel the mysteries that lurk within its abandoned halls.

Today, Royal Hope Hospital stands as a testament to the darker side of human history and the enduring fascination with the unknown. As the sun sets over the abandoned facility, casting long shadows across its decaying facade, one can't help but wonder what secrets still lie hidden within its walls and what restless spirits continue to wander its deserted corridors.

In the end, the true nature of the phenomena at Royal Hope Hospital may never be fully understood. Whether the hospital is a portal to the supernatural world, a manifestation of the collective human psyche, or simply an eerie relic of a bygone era, it remains an enigmatic and chilling presence in the annals of haunted hospitals. As visitors continue to be drawn to the site, hoping to catch a glimpse of the paranormal, the stories and legends surrounding Royal Hope Hospital will no doubt endure, adding yet another layer to the complex tapestry of human experience and our enduring fascination with the unknown.

Hirosaki City Hospital

Tucked away in the historic city of Hirosaki, in the northern Aomori Prefecture of Japan, lies a medical facility with a mysterious reputation. Hirosaki City Hospital, a seemingly ordinary institution dedicated to the healing of the body and mind, has become the subject of whispered conversations and fearful glances. The hospital's storied past and the numerous accounts of ghostly patients and paranormal encounters have etched it firmly into the annals of haunted medical facilities.

Originally established in the early 20th century, Hirosaki City Hospital has undergone multiple expansions and renovations over the years. Its long history and countless patients have left an indelible mark on the facility, and many believe that the spirits of those who passed away within its walls continue to roam the hallways, seeking solace in the afterlife.

One of the most famous stories associated with Hirosaki City Hospital is that of a young girl who is said to wander the paediatric wing. Numerous staff members and patients have reported seeing the small, forlorn figure, clad in a hospital gown, walking silently through the corridors. Some have even claimed to hear her plaintive cries echoing through the halls, as if searching for her family or seeking comfort in her final moments.

Another unsettling account involves a spectral figure known as the "White Lady." This ghostly apparition, thought to be a former nurse who worked at the hospital, has been witnessed by many, often in the dead of night. Cloaked in a white uniform, her face obscured by a veil, she is said to glide silently through the hospital, attending to her duties as if still tethered to the world of the living. Some have even reported feeling a gentle touch or the sensation of being watched, only to turn around and find the White Lady nearby, her gaze fixed on them with an inscrutable expression.

Perhaps the most chilling encounter at Hirosaki City Hospital is that of the "Phantom Elevator." Staff members working the night shift have reported hearing the soft hum of the elevator's machinery and the quiet ding of its arrival, despite the elevator being out of service. Upon investigation, the doors slide open to reveal an empty car, its lights flickering ominously. Some have even claimed to see ghostly figures standing within the elevator, their faces distorted and twisted with pain and anguish.

These paranormal encounters have not only been limited to the hospital's staff. Patients, too, have experienced their share of ghostly sightings and supernatural phenomena. One account tells of a patient who, upon waking from a fitful sleep, found herself staring into the eyes of a ghostly figure hovering above her bed. The apparition vanished as suddenly as it appeared, leaving the terrified patient questioning the boundaries between dreams and reality.

In addition to the ghostly patients and spectral nurses, there are also stories of inexplicable events taking place within Hirosaki City Hospital. Lights have been reported to flicker without explanation, and disembodied footsteps have been heard echoing through the empty corridors. Some have even reported the faint, lingering scent of antiseptic and disinfectant, as if the spirits of the past continue to maintain the hospital's once-sterile environment.

Sceptics argue that the stories surrounding Hirosaki City Hospital are little more than the products of overactive imaginations, fueled by the natural human tendency to fear the unknown. They maintain that the eerie atmosphere and the hospital's tragic history can easily lead individuals to interpret ordinary occurrences as supernatural in nature.

However, those who have experienced the unexplained phenomena at Hirosaki City Hospital firsthand insist that there is more to these encounters than mere coincidence or imagination. They argue that the hospital's long history of suffering and death has left an indelible imprint on the very fabric of the building, allowing the spirits of those who passed away within its walls to continue their existence in a liminal state between life and death. These restless souls, it is said, wander the hospital's corridors, still seeking healing and solace even as they remain forever tethered to the world of the living.

One particularly poignant story revolves around a former doctor who is believed to have taken his own life within the hospital. Overcome with grief and guilt after losing a young patient, he is said to have hung himself in one of the hospital's deserted rooms. Since then, his spirit has been reported to appear in the vicinity, a sorrowful figure shrouded in darkness and despair. Staff members who have encountered the tormented doctor often speak of the palpable sadness that permeates the air around him, leaving them with a lingering sense of melancholy long after the encounter.

Despite the unsettling tales and ghostly encounters, Hirosaki City Hospital continues to operate, providing much-needed medical care to the local community. While the hospital's reputation as a haunted medical facility has undoubtedly caused some unease among patients and staff alike, many have come to accept the supernatural phenomena as an inextricable part of the hospital's history and character.

As one delves into the eerie stories and chilling accounts that surround Hirosaki City Hospital, it becomes increasingly clear that the boundaries between the natural and the supernatural are not as clearly defined as one might think. The hospital stands as a testament to the human capacity for endurance and resilience, even in the face of unimaginable suffering and loss. The spirits that are said to haunt its halls serve as a reminder of the fragility of life and the indomitable power of the human spirit, which continues to persist even beyond the confines of death.

In the realm of the paranormal, Hirosaki City Hospital stands as a beacon of intrigue and fascination for those who seek to understand the mysteries of the afterlife. As more individuals share their spine-chilling encounters and inexplicable experiences within the hospital's hallowed halls, it becomes increasingly evident that the world of the supernatural is not as distant or unreachable as it may first appear. Instead, it seems to coexist alongside our everyday reality, a shadowy realm of restless spirits and unexplained phenomena that defies explanation and continues to captivate the imagination of those who dare to delve into the unknown.

Linda Vista Hospital

A former bustling medical centre, Linda Vista Hospital in Los Angeles, California, now stands as a silent sentinel of a forgotten era. This once-thriving institution, established in 1904, served the city's growing community until its closure in 1991. Since then, it has been transformed into a popular location for film and television productions. However, beyond the glamour of Hollywood, the hospital is reputed for its paranormal activity and ghostly encounters that have captivated the imagination of those who have dared to explore its abandoned halls.

The history of Linda Vista Hospital is riddled with tales of suffering and death. The facility initially catered to the healthcare needs of railroad employees and their families, but as the decades passed, the hospital expanded its services to the general public. The surrounding neighbourhood began to decline in the latter half of the 20th century, and with it, the hospital saw an increase in violence and traumatic injuries among its patients. This dark turn in its history is believed to have left an indelible mark on the building, resulting in the myriad of chilling encounters reported by those who have ventured inside its confines.

Many of the paranormal experiences at Linda Vista Hospital involve apparitions of former patients and medical staff, some of whom are believed to have met untimely ends within the hospital's walls. In the now-derelict surgery rooms, witnesses have reported seeing the spectral figure of a doctor, clad in bloodstained scrubs, moving purposefully through the area as if attending to a patient. This ghostly surgeon is said to be completely unaware of the living, focused solely on his eternal rounds.

A tragic tale surrounds the spirit of a young girl, whose presence has been noted in one of the hospital's empty patient rooms. This ethereal child, known as "Emily," is said to have died in the hospital after a failed surgery. Reports of her ghostly figure suggest a lonely, solemn presence, forever trapped within the confines of the medical facility. Her soft cries echo down the dimly lit corridors, as if calling out for comfort or solace.

Perhaps one of the most famous ghost sightings at Linda Vista Hospital involves the spectral figure of a nurse, spotted in the third-floor hallway. This enigmatic apparition, dressed in a white uniform reminiscent of a bygone era, has been witnessed by numerous visitors. She is described as having a solemn demeanour, walking silently down the hallway before disappearing into thin air. Some speculate that this ghostly nurse may be bound to the hospital due to an overwhelming sense of duty or guilt related to a tragic event in her past.

Linda Vista Hospital has also become notorious for its inexplicable cold spots and phantom sounds. Within the confines of the now-empty emergency room, there have been accounts of disembodied voices and blood-curdling screams echoing through the air. These chilling manifestations are believed to be the remnants of the hospital's tumultuous past, where life and death were in a constant struggle.

A notable paranormal investigation took place at Linda Vista Hospital in 2009, conducted by the television show "Ghost Adventures." During their stay, the investigators reported various unexplained phenomena, including strange noises, sudden drops in temperature, and disembodied voices. One investigator even claimed to have been physically attacked by an unseen force, which left him with scratches on his arm. The chilling experiences encountered by the "Ghost Adventures" crew only served to bolster the hospital's reputation as a paranormal hot spot.

While the ghostly encounters at Linda Vista Hospital may be frightening to some, others view these experiences as a window into the past, revealing the stories of those who once walked the hospital's halls. The spirits that are said to inhabit the building serve as a testament to the rich history of the hospital and the lives that were forever changed within its walls. For some, these spectral inhabitants offer a poignant reminder of the fleeting nature of life, while for others, they represent the enduring connection between the living and the departed.

The haunted reputation of Linda Vista Hospital continues to draw thrill-seekers, paranormal enthusiasts, and filmmakers to its crumbling façade. The hospital's eerie atmosphere has made it an ideal backdrop for numerous television shows and movies, including "Insidious: Chapter 2," "Pearl Harbor," "Buffy the Vampire Slayer," and "Dexter," among others. As a result, the hospital has become an iconic symbol of Hollywood's love affair with the macabre and the supernatural.

Despite its popularity as a filming location, those who have ventured inside Linda Vista Hospital often leave with a sense of unease, as if the building itself is imprinted with the emotional energy of its tragic past. The spectral figures that are said to roam its abandoned halls and the inexplicable occurrences that continue to be reported by visitors lend an air of mystery to this once-bustling medical facility.

As the sun sets and darkness descends upon the hospital, the shadows grow longer, and the chilling whispers of the past seem to grow ever louder. Those brave enough to explore the forsaken halls of Linda Vista Hospital are left to ponder the enigmatic presence of these lingering spirits, whose stories of life and death have become forever intertwined with the history of the building.

In the end, Linda Vista Hospital stands as a haunting reminder of the human experiences that once unfolded within its walls. The spectral inhabitants that are said to roam the premises reveal the indelible connection between the living and the dead, and the enduring power of the human spirit. As the stories of ghostly encounters and paranormal phenomena at Linda Vista Hospital continue to captivate the imagination, the hospital remains a testament to the power of the unknown and the enduring fascination with the world beyond our understanding.

Denbigh Mental Asylum

Located in the quaint Welsh countryside, the Denbigh Mental Asylum, also known as the North Wales Hospital, was once a place of refuge and healing for the mentally ill. Built in the mid-19th century, this once-bustling medical facility has been abandoned for decades and now stands as a haunting reminder of the suffering that transpired within its walls. The asylum's long history is marred by tales of abuse, neglect, and unimaginable pain, and the spirits of those who sought solace in its halls are believed to linger, creating an atmosphere ripe for paranormal activity and ghostly encounters.

Denbigh Mental Asylum was constructed between 1844 and 1848, with the intention of providing care for the mentally ill in Wales. The facility was designed in a Gothic Revival architectural style, with sprawling wards and intricate stonework that lent an air of dignity to the institution. At its peak, the hospital could house more than 1,500 patients, and it provided employment for many residents in the surrounding area. Over time, however, the treatment of patients within the asylum began to decline, and the once-noble institution became a place of despair and anguish.

By the mid-20th century, the reputation of Denbigh Mental Asylum had suffered considerably due to numerous reports of abuse, overcrowding, and poor living conditions for the patients. The facility was eventually shut down in 1995, and the buildings were left to decay, their windows shattered and their once-proud facades crumbling under the weight of time and neglect.

As the years have passed, stories of the paranormal activity within the asylum have spread, drawing the attention of paranormal investigators, urban explorers, and thrill-seekers alike. The ghostly residents of Denbigh Mental Asylum have been the subject of numerous eyewitness accounts, and the chilling tales of unexplained occurrences continue to captivate the imaginations of those who dare to explore the forsaken halls of the facility.

One of the most well-known spirits said to roam the halls of Denbigh Mental Asylum is that of a nurse known as Nurse Roberts. This spectral figure has been reported by multiple witnesses, who describe her as a woman in a nurse's uniform, appearing both solid and transparent. Nurse Roberts is often seen wandering the wards and corridors, as if still tending to the patients who once occupied the rooms.

In addition to the mysterious Nurse Roberts, visitors to the asylum have also reported encounters with a patient named Lily. Lily is described as a young woman, often seen in the children's ward, who appears to be searching for something or someone. Her presence is said to be accompanied by an overwhelming sense of sadness, and those who have witnessed her apparition often report feeling a deep empathy for the young woman.

Another unsettling account involves a ghostly figure known as the Faceless Man. The Faceless Man is often seen lurking in the shadows of the asylum, his features obscured by darkness. Witnesses describe him as a tall, gaunt figure, with a palpable sense of menace that seems to emanate from his very presence. The identity of the Faceless Man remains a mystery, but his chilling aura has left an indelible impression on those who have encountered him.

The abandoned wards and crumbling hallways of Denbigh Mental Asylum have also been the site of numerous reports of unexplained phenomena, including disembodied voices, footsteps echoing through empty rooms, and objects moving seemingly of their own accord. Paranormal investigators who have ventured into the depths of the asylum have recorded inexplicable sounds and captured images that defy rational explanation, fueling the belief that the spirits of the asylum's former inhabitants continue to dwell within the derelict facility.

The tragic history of Denbigh Mental Asylum is one that has left an indelible mark on the landscape of Wales, and the ghostly tales that have emerged from its abandoned halls serve as a chilling reminder of the suffering that transpired within its walls. The paranormal activity that continues to be reported by those who venture into the asylum has solidified its reputation as a haunted destination, drawing the curious and the brave from across the globe.

One particularly chilling account involves a group of paranormal investigators who visited the asylum to conduct a nighttime investigation. The team explored the various wards, recording sounds and attempting to communicate with the spirits believed to inhabit the facility. As they made their way through the crumbling hallways, the investigators reported an overwhelming sense of unease and dread that seemed to permeate the very air of the asylum.

The team's equipment began to malfunction, with batteries draining rapidly and recording devices inexplicably shutting off. As they continued their investigation, the team members began to experience physical sensations, such as the feeling of being touched or pushed by unseen forces. The investigators also reported hearing a chorus of disembodied voices, as if the spirits of the asylum were attempting to make their presence known.

In one particularly harrowing encounter, a member of the team witnessed a dark figure emerging from the shadows of a long-abandoned room. The figure appeared to be wearing a patient's gown and was hunched over as if in pain. The investigator watched in horror as the figure slowly approached, only to disappear suddenly when a flashlight was shone in its direction.

The experiences of the paranormal investigators, along with countless other eyewitness accounts, have contributed to the eerie legend of Denbigh Mental Asylum. These stories of ghostly encounters and unexplained phenomena have captivated the imaginations of those who are drawn to the dark corners of history, where the spirits of the past are believed to linger.

Today, the asylum stands as a decaying monument to the suffering and anguish that once filled its wards. Though time has taken its toll on the once-grand facility, the ghostly residents of Denbigh Mental Asylum continue to be the subject of fascination and fear for those who dare to delve into the tragic history of the institution.

As you immerse yourself in the chilling tales of Denbigh Mental Asylum, you may find yourself transported to the eerie, hallowed halls of the once-vibrant medical facility. With each account of ghostly apparitions and inexplicable occurrences, you will uncover the dark histories and chilling secrets that have transformed this asylum into a harrowing reminder of the past.

Prepare yourself for a spine-tingling journey into the shadowy world of haunted hospitals and asylums, where the stories of those who once sought healing and solace continue to echo through the forgotten corners of these forsaken institutions. Venture into the abandoned wards of Denbigh Mental Asylum, and delve deep into the world of the unknown, where the spirits of the tormented continue to roam, restless and unseen.

The Athens Lunatic Asylum

The Athens Lunatic Asylum, once a bustling hub of psychiatric care in Ohio, now stands as a testament to the darker side of medical history. With an eerie past that dates back to the late 19th century, this former mental health facility has gained notoriety for its chilling tales of paranormal activity and unexplained phenomena. Now part of Ohio University, the Athens Lunatic Asylum continues to cast a long shadow over the campus, its haunted legacy drawing in curious visitors and paranormal enthusiasts from all corners of the globe.

The asylum opened its doors in 1874, and for over a century, it served as a sanctuary for the mentally ill, offering care and treatment to those in need. However, as is the case with many institutions of its kind, the Athens Lunatic Asylum was not without its dark secrets. Lobotomies, electroconvulsive therapy, and other harsh treatments were commonly administered to patients, resulting in untold suffering and, in some cases, death.

With such a grim history, it is perhaps no surprise that the Athens Lunatic Asylum has become a hotbed of paranormal activity. Many believe that the spirits of former patients and staff continue to roam the facility's abandoned halls, their troubled souls seeking solace in the world of the living.

One of the most well-known stories from the asylum involves a patient named Margaret Schilling, who went missing in December 1978. Despite an extensive search, Margaret's body was not discovered until 42 days later when a maintenance worker found her lifeless form in an abandoned ward. The imprint of her body, along with a mysterious stain, remains etched into the floor of the room where she was found, serving as a haunting reminder of the tragedy that occurred within those walls.

Over the years, many visitors to the asylum have reported encountering Margaret's spirit. Some claim to have seen her wandering the halls, while others have heard her mournful cries echoing throughout the building. In addition to Margaret, numerous other ghostly apparitions have been reported, including those of former patients and staff members who are believed to be forever bound to the facility.

Eyewitness accounts of paranormal activity at the Athens Lunatic Asylum are not limited to mere sightings of apparitions. Many have experienced unexplained phenomena, such as sudden drops in temperature, disembodied voices, and the sensation of being touched or watched by unseen entities.

In one chilling account, a group of students from Ohio University ventured into the abandoned asylum in search of paranormal activity. Armed with cameras and recording equipment, they hoped to capture evidence of the supernatural. As they explored the dark, silent halls, the students reported feeling an overwhelming sense of unease, as if they were being watched from the shadows.

As the group made their way through the asylum, they began to hear strange noises, such as footsteps, whispers, and distant screams. At one point, a member of the group felt a cold hand on her shoulder, only to turn and find no one there. The students captured numerous EVP (electronic voice phenomenon) recordings during their investigation, including one particularly chilling message that seemed to say, "Get out."

The Athens Lunatic Asylum has also become a popular destination for seasoned paranormal investigators, who have documented a wide array of supernatural occurrences within its decaying walls. One such team, led by a renowned paranormal expert, conducted a thorough investigation of the facility and was astounded by the evidence they collected.

During their time at the asylum, the investigators witnessed numerous instances of unexplained phenomena, including mysterious orbs of light, moving shadows, and the sound of doors slamming shut on their own. In addition, they captured several EVP recordings, including one that appeared to be the voice of a former patient, crying out for help. In another recording, a voice could be heard whispering the name "Margaret," perhaps a reference to the tragic patient whose spirit is said to linger within the facility.

The paranormal experiences at the Athens Lunatic Asylum are not limited to the main building. The surrounding grounds, including the facility's cemetery, have also been the site of numerous ghostly encounters. Visitors to the cemetery have reported seeing apparitions of former patients, some of whom are believed to be buried in unmarked graves. In addition, many have experienced the sensation of being watched or followed while exploring the area.

One particularly unsettling account comes from a man who decided to visit the cemetery on a dare. As he walked among the gravestones, he began to hear the sound of footsteps following him. Despite searching the area, he could find no explanation for the noise. As he continued through the cemetery, the footsteps grew louder and more insistent, seemingly closing in on him. It was only when he left the grounds that the footsteps ceased, leaving him with the unnerving feeling that he had been pursued by something otherworldly.

The Athens Lunatic Asylum's haunted reputation has not only drawn in paranormal enthusiasts but also piqued the interest of the local community. Ohio University, which now encompasses the former asylum, has incorporated the facility's history into its educational programs, offering guided tours and lectures on the asylum's past.

These tours provide visitors with an opportunity to learn about the asylum's history, including its role in the treatment of mental illness and the controversial practices that were once commonplace within its walls. In addition, the tours offer participants a chance to explore the facility's abandoned wards and experience the eerie atmosphere that permeates the building.

The Athens Lunatic Asylum stands as a chilling reminder of the darker side of medical history, its haunted halls echoing with the voices of those who once sought solace within its walls. For those who dare to explore its decaying corridors, the asylum offers a glimpse into a world where the line between the living and the dead is anything but clear, and the tormented souls of the past continue to roam, seeking solace in the world of the living.

As you reflect on the chilling tales of the Athens Lunatic Asylum and the many other haunted hospitals and asylums chronicled in this volume, you may find yourself questioning the nature of reality and the boundaries that separate life and death. In these hallowed halls of suffering and healing, the restless spirits of those who have gone before us serve as a haunting reminder of the fragile nature of our existence and the enduring power of the human spirit.

Edinburgh's Royal Hospital for Sick Children

In the historic city of Edinburgh, Scotland, stands the Royal Hospital for Sick Children, a renowned paediatric facility with a legacy of healing and hope that dates back to its founding in 1860. Over the years, the hospital has provided care and treatment for countless children, earning a reputation as a beacon of hope in the community. However, the hospital's storied history is not without its share of ghostly encounters and paranormal activity. Tales of healing spirits, phantom nurses, and other supernatural phenomena have become intertwined with the hospital's legacy, adding an air of intrigue and mystery to this revered institution.

One of the most enduring legends associated with the Royal Hospital for Sick Children is that of the "Blue Lady," a spectral figure believed to be the spirit of a former nurse who continues to watch over the hospital's young patients. Clad in a blue uniform, this ethereal figure has been spotted by numerous staff members and patients alike, her presence often accompanied by a comforting sense of calm and reassurance.

In one particularly poignant account, a young patient recovering from a serious illness awoke in the middle of the night to find the Blue Lady sitting at the foot of her bed. The ghostly nurse gently reassured the child that she was on the path to recovery, and that she would always be there to watch over her. The next morning, the young patient excitedly recounted her encounter with the Blue Lady, much to the astonishment of the hospital staff, who were well acquainted with the spirit's legend.

In addition to the Blue Lady, the hospital is also said to be home to the spirit of a young girl named Sarah, who is believed to have passed away within its walls. Dressed in a white nightgown and with a playful demeanour, Sarah is often seen wandering the hospital's halls, particularly in areas near the former children's ward. Many staff members have reported encounters with this playful spirit, who seems to take delight in surprising and interacting with those who cross her path.

One nurse, working the night shift, was startled to find a young girl in a white nightgown standing in an empty corridor. As she approached the child to ask if she was lost, the girl suddenly vanished into thin air, leaving the bewildered nurse to ponder her ghostly encounter. In another account, a janitor who was mopping the floors late at night claimed to have heard the sound of children's laughter, only to turn around and find a small, translucent girl in a white nightgown grinning at him before disappearing as suddenly as she had appeared.

But the tales of ghostly activity at the Royal Hospital for Sick Children do not end with the Blue Lady and Sarah. Numerous staff members and visitors have reported a wide array of unexplained phenomena, from disembodied footsteps and the sound of children's laughter to mysterious orbs of light and sudden drops in temperature.

One staff member recounted a chilling encounter in the hospital's basement, where she had been sent to retrieve some supplies. As she navigated the dimly lit corridors, she began to hear the unmistakable sound of a child sobbing. As she followed the sound, she came upon a small, spectral figure huddled in the corner, weeping inconsolably. The staff member reached out to comfort the child, only for the apparition to vanish before her eyes.

Some paranormal investigators who have ventured into the hospital in search of evidence of the supernatural have come away with a wealth of intriguing findings. During one such investigation, a team of experienced ghost hunters was astonished to capture an EVP (electronic voice phenomenon) recording of a child's voice, singing a haunting lullaby. Other investigators have reported capturing images of ghostly figures and orbs of light on their cameras, further fueling the belief that the Royal Hospital for Sick Children is indeed home to a number of healing spirits and ghostly inhabitants.

Despite the chilling nature of these encounters, many staff members and visitors to the hospital view the presence of these spirits as a source of comfort and reassurance. The Blue Lady, Sarah, and the other ghostly residents are seen as guardian angels, watching over the young patients and providing a sense of hope and solace during their time of need.

In one heartwarming tale, a young boy undergoing treatment for a life-threatening illness confided in his nurse that he had been visited by a kind, ethereal woman dressed in blue. According to the boy, the Blue Lady had spent the night at his bedside, soothing him and assuring him that he would soon be well again. As the boy recovered and prepared to leave the hospital, he insisted that the Blue Lady had played a crucial role in his healing process, providing him with the strength and courage to face his illness head-on.

The Royal Hospital for Sick Children, with its long history of providing care and healing to the children of Edinburgh and beyond, serves as a testament to the enduring power of hope and the resilience of the human spirit. The tales of ghostly nurses and healing spirits that abound within its walls speak to a deeper connection between the living and the dead, where love, compassion, and the desire to heal transcend the boundaries of time and space.

Sai Ying Pun Psychiatry Hospital

Hong Kong, a bustling metropolis known for its towering skyscrapers, vibrant street markets, and fusion of Eastern and Western cultures, hides a dark and chilling secret. Amidst the urban landscape, Sai Ying Pun Psychiatry Hospital stands as a testament to the city's turbulent past and the lingering presence of the paranormal. Its haunted halls and ghostly patients evoke an unsettling atmosphere that continues to send shivers down the spines of those who dare to explore its foreboding corridors.

Established in the early 20th century, Sai Ying Pun Psychiatry Hospital was initially intended as a sanctuary for those afflicted by mental illness. However, the hospital's history is marred by tales of questionable treatments, overcrowding, and the alleged abuse of patients. As the years went by, the hospital's reputation grew darker, with stories of unexplained occurrences and paranormal activity beginning to emerge.

One such tale involves a nurse named Ling, who worked the night shift at the hospital during the 1970s. As she made her rounds one evening, she encountered a patient who seemed to be in severe distress, muttering incoherently and clutching his head in pain. Ling attempted to console the man and administer medication, but as she reached out to touch him, her hand passed right through his body. Startled, she realised that the patient before her was no longer among the living. This harrowing encounter was just the beginning of a series of ghostly sightings and eerie experiences that plagued the hospital.

Visitors and staff have reported encountering the apparitions of former patients, their hollow eyes and forlorn expressions a haunting reminder of the suffering that took place within the hospital's walls. In one chilling account, a doctor claimed to have seen a group of spectral patients gathered in a long-disused therapy room, as if they were waiting for a session that would never come. Their ghostly whispers filled the air, sending shivers down the doctor's spine as he hastily retreated from the unsettling scene.

In addition to the tormented spirits of former patients, the restless souls of the hospital's staff are also said to roam the premises. A former orderly named Mr. Wong recounts a bone-chilling experience in which he encountered the spectre of a long-deceased nurse. As he walked the dimly lit halls late one night, he heard the unmistakable sound of footsteps following him. Turning around, he saw the apparition of a nurse in a tattered and bloodstained uniform, her gaze fixed upon him with an intensity that sent chills down his spine. Despite his terror, Mr. Wong could not help but feel a sense of profound sadness emanating from the spirit, as if she were trapped in an eternal cycle of despair.

The chilling history of Sai Ying Pun Psychiatry Hospital has given rise to numerous legends, including the infamous "Room 21." According to local lore, this room was the site of horrific experiments and treatments, with patients subjected to electroconvulsive therapy and other painful procedures in a misguided attempt to cure their mental afflictions. It is said that the screams of the tortured can still be heard echoing through the halls at night, and that those who venture too close to Room 21 risk being confronted by the anguished spirits of the patients who suffered within its walls.

The hospital's sinister reputation has attracted the attention of paranormal investigators and thrill-seekers alike, many of whom have attempted to explore its haunted halls in search of definitive proof of the supernatural. Some have claimed to have captured ghostly figures on film, while others have recorded eerie voices and unexplained sounds. While sceptics may dismiss these findings as mere fabrications or the product of overactive imaginations, the sheer volume of encounters and the consistency of the reports lend a certain credibility to the notion that something otherworldly lurks within the hospital's walls.

As the sun sets and darkness envelops the city, Sai Ying Pun Psychiatry Hospital takes on an even more foreboding atmosphere. Shadows cast by the moonlight dance across the crumbling facade, creating an eerie backdrop for the spectral inhabitants who are said to roam the halls. Venturing into the hospital at night is a chilling experience, with the creaking floorboards, distant moans, and faint whispers of the unseen residents adding to the sense of unease.

One particularly harrowing account comes from a group of urban explorers who ventured into the hospital after hours, armed with flashlights and cameras in the hopes of capturing evidence of the paranormal. As they made their way through the decaying wards, they were startled by the sudden sound of footsteps echoing through the empty halls. The footsteps grew louder and more insistent, as if an unseen entity was in pursuit. Panicked, the group fled the hospital, vowing never to return.

In recent years, Sai Ying Pun Psychiatry Hospital has gained notoriety as a hotspot for ghost hunters and paranormal enthusiasts, who flock to the site in search of the unexplained. The hospital's haunted halls continue to captivate the imaginations of those who dare to venture within, with countless individuals eager to bear witness to the ghostly patients and eerie occurrences that are said to pervade the premises.

Despite the countless testimonies and chilling encounters, the true extent of the paranormal activity at Sai Ying Pun Psychiatry Hospital remains shrouded in mystery. As the hospital's haunted legacy endures, the stories of ghostly patients and sinister occurrences continue to captivate those who are drawn to the world of the supernatural. As the boundaries between the living and the dead become ever more blurred within the haunted halls of this notorious medical facility, one thing remains certain: the restless spirits of Sai Ying Pun Psychiatry Hospital will continue to haunt the memories of those who have dared to explore its dark and chilling past.

Lier Sykehus

The haunting silence that envelops Lier Sykehus, an abandoned asylum located in the picturesque countryside of Norway, belies the chilling past that once unfolded within its forsaken halls. This once-bustling institution, which opened its doors in 1926, was dedicated to the treatment and care of the mentally ill. However, as the years went by, the asylum's history became tainted with stories of inhumane treatment, forced lobotomies, and untold suffering, ultimately leading to its closure in 1986.

With the passage of time, Lier Sykehus has become a ghostly shell of its former self, its decaying corridors and empty wards serving as a stark reminder of the pain and anguish that once permeated its walls. The stories of paranormal phenomena and ghostly encounters that have emerged from this forsaken institution continue to captivate the imaginations of those who are drawn to the world of the supernatural, and today, the asylum stands as a chilling testament to the restless spirits who are said to linger within its desolate confines.

Visitors to Lier Sykehus often speak of a palpable sense of unease that seems to pervade the very air, as if the tortured souls of former patients continue to cry out for solace and understanding. The asylum's eerie atmosphere is further heightened by the chilling reports of unexplained phenomena and ghostly encounters that have been witnessed by those brave enough to venture within its walls. From disembodied voices to shadowy figures that seem to flit through the darkness, the asylum's haunted legacy continues to unfold, captivating the minds and hearts of those who seek to unravel its dark and chilling secrets.

One such account comes from a group of paranormal investigators who, drawn by the asylum's sinister reputation, decided to explore the abandoned institution in search of the supernatural. Armed with cameras, audio recorders, and an unwavering determination to uncover the truth, the group ventured into the asylum's decaying halls, little knowing the chilling encounters that awaited them.

As the investigators made their way through the derelict wards, they were startled by the sudden sound of a door slamming shut, followed by the eerie creaking of floorboards as if someone or something was moving through the darkness. Undeterred, the group continued their exploration, only to be confronted by the chilling sight of a shadowy figure that seemed to appear out of nowhere, its dark form flickering and vanishing as quickly as it had materialised.

The chilling encounters did not end there, however. As the night wore on, the investigators were continually confronted by a series of inexplicable occurrences, from the disembodied sound of laughter echoing through the empty corridors to the sudden and unexplained movement of objects within the asylum's forsaken rooms. It soon became clear to the group that they were not alone within the haunted halls of Lier Sykehus, and that the restless spirits of the institution's tormented past were still very much present within its chilling confines.

Another unsettling account comes from a local resident who, drawn by curiosity and the asylum's haunted reputation, decided to explore the abandoned institution on a cold winter's night. As the intrepid adventurer made his way through the darkened corridors, he was struck by the overwhelming sense of sadness and despair that seemed to hang in the air like a heavy shroud.

As he ventured deeper into the asylum, the man was startled by the sudden sound of footsteps echoing through the darkness, their ghostly cadence growing louder and more insistent as if someone was following him through the gloomy halls. As he turned to confront the unseen pursuer, the man was confronted by the chilling sight of a shadowy figure that seemed to dissolve into the darkness as he watched, leaving him with a sense of inexplicable dread that would haunt him for years to come.

Yet another eerie account comes from a woman who, along with a group of friends, decided to explore the abandoned asylum in search of adventure and the supernatural. As they cautiously made their way through the darkened halls, the group was startled by the sudden sound of a woman's voice, the disembodied words echoing through the silence as if calling out to them from beyond the grave.

Drawn by the ghostly voice, the group ventured deeper into the asylum, only to be confronted by a series of unexplained phenomena that left them questioning the very nature of reality. From the chilling sensation of being touched by unseen hands to the eerie sound of footsteps echoing in the darkness behind them, the group was left with no doubt that they were not alone within the haunted halls of Lier Sykehus.

These chilling encounters are just a few of the countless stories that have emerged from the forsaken asylum, each tale adding another layer of mystery and intrigue to the institution's haunted legacy. As the years have passed, the once-bustling halls of Lier Sykehus have become a chilling testament to the suffering and anguish that once unfolded within its walls, the ghostly echoes of its dark and tragic past continuing to resonate through the desolate corridors and empty wards.

While the true nature of the supernatural phenomena that seem to pervade the abandoned asylum may never be fully understood, one thing is certain: the restless spirits of Lier Sykehus continue to linger within its forsaken halls, their tormented cries a haunting reminder of the chilling past that refuses to be forgotten.

Today, Lier Sykehus stands as a desolate monument to the dark and tragic history that unfolded within its walls, its decaying corridors and empty wards serving as a chilling reminder of the suffering and torment that once permeated its forsaken halls. As the chilling tales of ghostly encounters and unexplained phenomena continue to captivate the imaginations of those drawn to the world of the supernatural, the abandoned asylum remains a haunting testament to the restless spirits who are said to linger within its desolate confines, their cries for solace and understanding echoing through the silence like a mournful dirge.

As you ponder the chilling accounts and dark history that surround Lier Sykehus, you may find yourself wondering what secrets still lie hidden within its haunted halls, their ghostly whispers calling out to you from beyond the veil of time and memory. And as you immerse yourself in the chilling tales of the paranormal that continue to unfold within this forsaken institution, you may find that the true horror lies not in the supernatural phenomena that seem to pervade its abandoned wards, but in the tragic and all-too-human stories of suffering and anguish that unfolded within its walls, their echoes still reverberating through the silence like the distant cries of the damned.

As you conclude your journey through the haunted world of Lier Sykehus, you may find that the chilling encounters and dark history that have come to define this forsaken asylum serve as a powerful reminder of the thin line that separates the world of the living from the realm of the dead, their ghostly echoes a haunting testament to the restless spirits who continue to wander the shadowy halls of this abandoned institution, their cries for solace and understanding forever lost within the darkness.

Afterword

As we reach the end of our spine-tingling journey through "Haunted Hospitals: Ghostly Encounters and Paranormal Phenomena in Medical Facilities," we are left with a profound sense of the complex relationship between life and death, and the enduring mysteries that continue to mystify us. From the hallowed halls of Waverly Hills Sanatorium to the forsaken corridors of Lier Sykehus, we have delved deep into the shadowy realms of medical institutions across the globe, where the line between the living and the dead is said to be at its most fragile.

In traversing these haunted landscapes, we have borne witness to the countless stories of suffering and anguish that unfolded within the walls of these once-vibrant institutions, their chilling echoes still reverberating through the abandoned wards and desolate corridors. We have encountered the restless spirits and ghostly apparitions that are said to linger within these forsaken buildings, their haunting cries for solace and understanding a stark reminder of the tragic pasts that continue to haunt these eerie locales.

As we reflect upon the chilling tales and unnerving encounters that have characterised our exploration of these haunted hospitals and asylums, we are reminded of the enduring power of the human spirit, its ability to transcend the boundaries of life and death in search of understanding and redemption. We have seen firsthand the impact that these ghostly encounters can have on those who dare to delve into the realm of the paranormal, their lives forever changed by the supernatural phenomena that they have witnessed within the haunted confines of these medical facilities.

While the stories and experiences recounted in this book may defy logical explanation, they serve as a powerful testament to the deep-seated human fascination with the unknown, the mysterious, and the inexplicable. In a world that is increasingly defined by rational thought and scientific inquiry, it is perhaps this very fascination that continues to draw us towards the haunted hospitals and asylums of our past, their chilling tales and ghostly encounters offering a tantalising glimpse into the uncharted realms that lie beyond the veil of our understanding.

As we bring our journey through the haunted world of medical institutions to a close, it is our hope that you, the reader, have been left with a deeper appreciation of the enigmatic nature of the supernatural, and the enduring mysteries that continue to captivate our collective imagination. Whether you are a believer in the paranormal, a seeker of the unknown, or simply a lover of chilling tales and eerie encounters, we trust that you have found something to captivate your imagination within the pages of this haunting compendium.

As you step back into the world beyond the haunted halls and forsaken wards of these once-revered medical facilities, may you carry with you a newfound sense of wonder and curiosity, a reminder of the enduring mysteries that still lie hidden within the shadowy recesses of our world. And as you reflect upon the chilling tales and ghostly encounters that have come to define the haunted legacy of these hospitals and asylums, may you find solace in the knowledge that, in the realm of the paranormal, the boundaries between life and death, the natural and the supernatural, are never quite as clear-cut as they may seem.

In closing, we thank you for joining us on this unsettling journey into the heart of darkness, where the spirits of those who once sought healing and solace continue to roam, restless and unseen. May the chilling stories and haunting encounters that have come to define the world of haunted hospitals and asylums serve as a powerful reminder of the enduring mysteries that continue to surround us, their ghostly echoes a haunting testament to the complex relationship between life and death, and the enigmatic nature of the human spirit.

The End.

To read more books by this author, just search "Lee Brickley" on Amazon!

Printed in Great Britain
by Amazon